To E. [...]
"Up [...]
Russell M. College[...]
Phil 3: 12-14

The
Boy
from
the
Barn

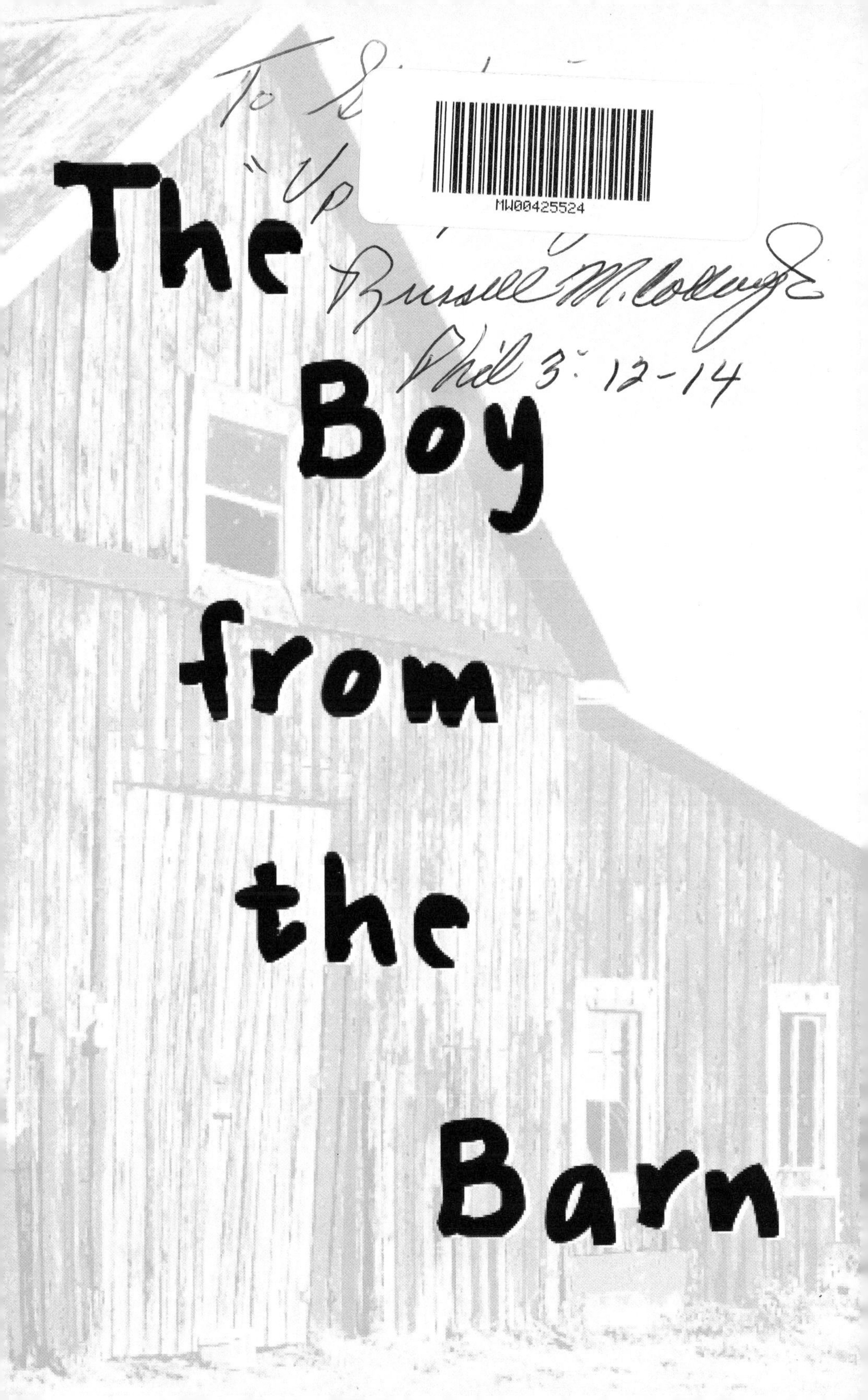

Copyright Page

Russell McCollough
PO Box 1149
Roseville, CA 95678

russellmccollough.com
russell.mccollough@gmail.com

The Boy from the Barn
by Russell McCollough

ISBN #978-1490382739
Cover and Design by Christa Proctor

Dedication

I dedicate this book to my wife, Judy, who for the past forty-five years has been the rock I lean on and my shelter from the storms.

Acknowledgments

I have been blessed to have a wonderful family and a host of friends – young and old. It is my pleasure to acknowledge some who have helped me in my journey through life.

First, I would like to express appreciation to my family for their love and commitment. To my wife Judy, daughters Christa and Angela, sons-in-law, Don and Marc and my lovely grandchildren – Ashley, Danielle, Caelan, Sophia, Aidan, Victoria and Annalise – you have all brought me joy and helped me have a sense of wholeness. Thank you for your love toward me.

To other family members and friends who have stood with me through the good and the bad – you have been the instruments God has used to help shape me. Many are special but I must name a few that stand out brightly upon the tapestry of my life.

The Keener, Davis and Vincent Families – your love and encouragement have been more precious than gold.

Charlie and Sue Cagle – thank you for the years of laughter, good times, constant friendship and the gift of your love and service to our church family.

Art and Rachel Quezada – Art has been promoted but his spirit lives on in his family and through all those to whom he imparted his life and love. May God bless you for your friendship, unwavering loyalty and encouragement.

Bill and Missy Taylor – Thank you for your genuine love and support even when your children were young and your hands were full. The fruit of your labor is evident in the lives of your amazing offspring.

A Personal Note from the Author

Every life is a journey. This is the story of my journey. Although some of the details in this book could be written from a different perspective by those who shared my life, this is my story based on my particular recollections.

The Boy from the Barn is a true story. When I was eight years old, my family was basically homeless, living in a barn in the little farming community of Seville near Ivanhoe, California. By the time I turned nine, I was no longer attending school and my life was in jeopardy due to a lack of food and the basic necessities of life. Thankfully, I was rescued from this nightmare and over a period of time experienced a miraculous recovery.

Due to the remarkable changes in my life, I was able to achieve success in my health, family and career. Later, I would come to the realization that although I had experienced transformation physically and mentally, a "bruise" remained in my soul.

Long after an individual suffers physical, emotional and mental abuse, a residue of the pain may remain, causing the individual to believe lies about themselves. Some part of that lie will tell you that your future has no hope and your expectations of security may never be realized. You may be able to "hide" the bruises experienced in life but the pain in your soul will remind you the bruise is still there.

Through trials and failures, I found freedom from the "bruise" that I had received in my early childhood. The principles that have helped me to sustain this freedom are found in Chapter 19 of this book – "Maintaining Your Liberty."

This is a story that will make you cry but will also make you laugh. It is my sincere hope that you will realize the following truth: ***You never have to be down, you can always be up or getting up.***

Table of Contents

Chapter 1 – The Early Years

I was born on September 18, 1945 - the sixth of seven children born to Mauren and Doris McCollough. Darlene was the oldest – then Dale, Charles, Gwen, Laura, Russell (me) and Louise.

There is very little I remember about the earliest years of my life. Based on family photos, it appears that our home life had some sort of stability during those years. I have seen pictures of clean, attractive brothers and sisters. However, by the time I was age nine, my constant companions were hunger, fear, loneliness and sickness. The bare necessities common to most families in America were unknown to me.

The primary reason for my sad, dysfunctional living condition was due to the fact that my parents were alcoholics. It seemed as though they had one purpose in life – to drink as much as possible. Looking back upon that time, I now realize they were most likely wounded people who had turned to alcohol in order to numb hurts they had sustained in their own lives. Not that their behavior could be excused but perhaps they had circumstances that would forever remain unknown to me.

By the year 1953, there was little stability in our lives as our family moved into a different rental house every few months in the little country towns of Woodlake and Ivanhoe, California.

By the time I was eight years old, we no longer lived in a

house but in an old, abandoned barn on the outskirts of Ivanhoe in a little community known as Seville. This barn was our dwelling place – certainly not a home. The barn did not come with running water, bathroom facilities or utility hookups. The only water available to us came from an outside hydrant about a block away from the barn. I don't think bathing was a priority to me during this time – it was just too inconvenient for one small hungry boy to carry that many buckets of water.

Even though my father resided in the places we called home, he was absent most of the time. He was either working as a farm laborer or he was in the beer tavern drinking until he was wasted. When he finally made his way home at night, he would be drunk. I became very familiar with the smell of tobacco and alcohol.

Upon my father's return from the tavern, we could be sure of one thing – he would wake up the whole family, insist we get out of bed, demand everyone's attention and begin verbally abusing the oldest child. Most of the confrontations that I observed took place between my father and my sister Gwen, who at the time was 12 years old.

My two oldest siblings had been fortunate enough to leave home – Dale joined the Navy and Darlene had moved in with our maternal grandparents in Madera. Although Charles remained at home, he was of an age to be out and about – therefore, his presence in our home during this period is not prominent in my memories.

Before Darlene left home, she bore the brunt of my father's angry conversations. By the time I turned five years old, she was no longer in the home so Dad's anger was primarily vented upon Gwen. I have no recollection of my mother attempting to intervene during these times. Perhaps she was indisposed due to her own drinking, or maybe she had tried to intervene in the past and found that her efforts were in vain.

I had one thing to be very thankful for – my father didn't seem to be prone to violent physical behavior – at least toward me. To my recollection, he didn't beat us – in fact, I don't recall receiving so much as a spanking from either one of my parents.

Neglect and fear were my constant companions. Thoughts of happiness were foreign to me – there was a lack of hope and no expectation of a better life.

During the daylight hours, most of my time was spent sitting in the car with Gwen, Laura and Louise while our parents were drinking inside a bar. Sometimes I would walk up and down the streets of Ivanhoe trying to find coke and beer bottles to recycle for cash. In those days, you could get five cents for the larger coke bottles (party pak) and three cents for the smaller ones. Five cents would buy a candy bar or a package of chips.

My pleasures in life were few but like most little boys, I attempted to find enjoyment in the small adventures that came my way.

I had a special place that I considered my very own spot where I could sit and watch the traffic go by. It was a large boulder about four feet high located at the side of the road. From my perch atop this boulder, I would look for large trucks coming down the road. When I caught sight of a truck, I would begin pumping my little fist in the air trying desperately to get the driver to notice me and blow his air horn. When I was successful in gaining my desired result, I would become excited and begin jumping up and down. This little activity added a sense of victory and accomplishment to my day.

Once when I was around five years old, I was sitting on this large boulder when the thought came into my mind that I should get off and move away. After I was about 20 feet from the rock, a driver lost control of his car and slammed into the rock, totaling his vehicle. There is not a doubt in my mind that if I had remained on the rock, I would have been seriously injured or perhaps killed. Although I didn't realize it until years later, it was probably the first time I had a real awareness of the voice of God as it had most surely been a higher power impressing me to move away from the rock.

In my younger years I suffered from occasional bouts of severe earaches. As I mentioned earlier, there is little I remember about my early life, but I do remember those painful earaches.

One night, as was common to our family, my parents decided to go out to the bar and drink. I was around three years old at the time. The responsibility to stay home and care for the younger children that evening fell upon Dale, who was 11 years older than me which would have made him about 14. My earaches were a common occurrence three or four times each month. My temperature would rise to a very high level and I would become delirious and fall in and out of consciousness. This particular evening I was also vomiting and coughing up blood.

While my siblings huddled together and cried, Dale held me as he blew cigarette smoke into my ear in an attempt to relieve the pain. Not knowing what to do, he offered me a drink of water and then wiped my face with a cold cloth. I remember him crying and yelling for my parents to come home. Of course they didn't come for what seemed like hours and when they did, they were drunk. They didn't bother taking me to the doctor.

In later years, Darlene told me she recalled that on one occasion she begged my parents to take me to the doctor for my earache and high fever. Apparently, they did put me in the car and drove away and she assumed they were taking me for medical attention. However, later she realized they left me in the car while they stopped at a beer joint to drink. I never made it to the doctor that time either.

In Dale's late teenage years he made the decision to join the Navy. I missed him during those years and looked forward with excitement and great anticipation to the times he would come home on leave for a few days.

Louise was the youngest of all the children. When I think back on that time of my life, I remember mine and Louise's relationship and think of what might have been had things worked out differently. She was my little buddy and playmate. When I was seven and she was six, we would often play with wooden blocks outside in the dirt, pretending the blocks were little cars.

Then, there were times we would take an old automobile tire or bicycle rim and roll them around the yard. My brother Dale, who had quite a sense of humor, saw us playing one day when he was home on leave from the Navy. He had a great time teasing me, saying, "Russell, you look like a little Ford coupe going down the road with both doors open." He was referring to my big ears that stuck out prominently from the sides of my head.

One experience with Louise stands out very clearly in my mind. I was in the first grade and Louise was in kindergarten. It was early morning and we were waiting for the school bus on the side of the road. The house we lived in at the time was set off the road and out of view. As we stood there, a car with four flashy adults – two men and two women – stopped by and offered us a ride to school. Not knowing the danger we were in and not having the advantage of proper training in how to avoid strangers, we agreed to get into the car.

We were driven around for a few minutes and then the car began to head out of town. We became frightened and started screaming and crying. In response to our crying, these individuals took out some long knives and began to display them to us.

I guess they thought what was interesting and entertaining to them would somehow console us. Of course that did not help our state of mind – it only served to cause our kicking and screaming to intensify. Finally they turned around and took us to our school and dropped us off a block away. I walked into my first grade classroom and of course I was late. The teacher wanted to know why and after I explained what happened, she rushed me to the principal's office.

Louise was brought in as well and we repeated the story of what had happened. Later that afternoon, we were taken back to the principal's office. When we got there, three policemen and the four individuals that had taken us for the unwanted ride were waiting for us.

We immediately became frightened and began crying but were able to confirm that these were the four people that had taken us for the ride. I never learned what happened to them. I do remember that my parents acted as though it was no big deal. Perhaps it was their way of trying to help us remain calm.

As time went by, my family's living situation continued to decline. The four children remaining at home – Gwen, Laura, myself and Louise were not doing well physically or mentally. Eventually, we attracted the attention of the county welfare department. Social workers would regularly come to our school and remove us from classes for a lunch break.

Either they had been informed that we were not eating well or it was apparent by looking at us because they would take us to the local grocery store in order to buy our lunch.

In those days grocery stores didn't have nice deli areas with tables and chairs so the social worker would purchase bread and lunchmeat and make sandwiches right there in the store. We were then expected to eat our sandwich as other customers walked by and stared. Although it could have been embarrassing and possibly was to my older siblings, I was simply glad to have food in my belly.

By the time I was nine years old I weighed 31 pounds – about one half the average weight for a boy of that age. I was no longer attending school and was basically homeless; literally living out of trash cans, sleeping in the barn at night.

It's amazing what a child will do to try and get some food to fill their empty stomach. There were times when I would try to concoct my own delicacies. On one occasion I observed a Mexican family cooking a meal out of cactus which they grew in their yard. Of course, I didn't have the menu nor did I understand the method of preparing and cooking such a meal but my hunger drove me to try and do something.

First, I gathered some wood I found laying around outside the barn, picked up some matches – which we always had in abundance due to my parents being smokers – and proceeded to build a fire. Then, I found an old empty tin can; cut up the cactus in little squares, added some water and tried to boil it in the can. It tasted terrible. However, I was able to swallow a couple of bites. Wow! That was awful. I forced it down thinking that if the Mexicans could eat it, so could I. Let me assure you – it tasted worse coming back up than it did going down.

On another occasion, I found some flour and decided I would cook up some biscuits. I made some dough by mixing the flour with water. I then took a small, open tin can and cut out some biscuits and laid them on a tin pie pan to cook. I noticed they were about to burn so I took them off the fire. They were still doughy but I decided to go ahead and eat them anyway. Once again, my delicacy tasted worse coming up than it did going down. To this day, I have a bad association with eating anything that appears doughy, including dumplings and soggy bread.

Even if adequate food supplies had been available to us – which they were not – it would have been difficult to prepare proper meals in the barn. Having no utilities, the barn was cold during the winter and hot in the summer. We had to walk quite a distance to get into town and often we were left alone at the barn while our parents went about their business – such as it was.

Chapter 2 – Rescued from Certain Death

One night in December 1954, a lady I recognized but had little acquaintance with, came into the barn. I would later learn she had noticed me the previous day as I was walking up and down the streets of Ivanhoe. After one long look at me, she had become very concerned about my welfare. Based on my appearance, she realized I didn't stand a chance if someone didn't intervene on my behalf.

After she saw me that day, she went home from work, told her husband she had seen me walking the streets of Ivanhoe, and explained how dirty and sickly I was. Then, she asked if he would be willing to let her bring me home to live with them if my parents would allow it. He immediately gave her permission to seek out my parents to see what she could do for me.

Since she worked in a packing house in Ivanhoe, she determined that once she got off work, she would try and find me. She inquired of people in the area where she had seen me asking, "Do you know where the little boy named Russell lives?"

Soon, she got a response. Someone told her, "Yes, he lives in a barn just outside of town." With a little effort she was able to determine the location of the barn as being in the Seville area.

I remember that evening very well. My mother happened to be in the barn that night. I saw this well dressed lady come into the barn and then heard her say, "Is it okay if I take Russell home to live with me?" Not knowing her, I began to whine and cry.

Despite my protests, I heard my mother say, "Yes you can have him." Then, my mother put a few belongings in a bag and handed me off to this lady who was basically a stranger to me.

Even though my living situation was dire, you may well understand that it broke my heart to realize my own mother was giving me away. I was devastated by her words – "Yes, you can have him." It was like a dagger piercing my heart. Little did I know, I would not see my mother again for several years and then only for one brief visit. It is my understanding that shortly after she gave me away, she left my father and lived a transient life on her own.

Later in life I came to understand that my mother's decision to give me away was probably based on her belief it would be best for me. But at the time, all I could think was – *my mother is giving me away to a stranger.*

The lady who rescued me from certain death and who I barely knew, turned out to be a wonderful, loving person named Ruth McCollough. She was my aunt by marriage – her husband, my Uncle Ralph, was my father's brother. She would turn out to be a *real mother* to me.

But that sad evening in the barn, the scared little nine year old boy was resistant and tearful. In spite of this, Aunt Ruth put me in her car even while I continued to cry as we headed out to our destination. It was dark when we arrived at her home. When we walked in, my Uncle Ralph got his first glimpse of me and began crying.

They fed me, gave me a bath, put one of their clean shirts on me and decided to let me sleep with them that first night. I wasn't able to sleep because I continued to cry throughout the night.

The following morning Aunt Ruth took me to the barber shop and then we went shopping for new clothes. Next, she took me to the doctor for a physical examination. She knew I was in very poor health and the doctor confirmed that in addition to being severely malnourished, I had also lost most of the hearing in my left ear. His medical prognosis was all doom and gloom.

He said, "Mrs. McCollough, this boy is in very poor health. I don't expect him to last more than a few weeks. It's my belief that you will be getting a funeral bill if you choose to take responsibility for him."

Thankfully, Aunt Ruth was a woman of faith who refused to follow the advice of the doctor. She took me home and began doing everything in her power to get me well. She fed me nourishing food from her garden, lovingly cared for me and enrolled me in school. After living in their home for awhile, I came to understand Aunt Ruth and Uncle Ralph had a loving, caring relationship and both were dedicated church going, Bible believing Christians.

It was one week before Christmas when I went to live with my aunt and uncle. On the Sunday before Christmas, we attended church together for the first time as a family.

Aunt Ruth was the teacher of my age group's Sunday school class. On the previous Sunday the students had drawn names in order to have a gift exchange. Because I was not in attendance when the class drew names, I did not have a gift to give anyone nor did I expect to receive one. However, there was a boy in the class whose name I would later find out was Dwight Herron. We had not yet been introduced so I had no idea he was Aunt Ruth's sister's son. This meant that he was now my cousin. I could tell that he was very popular and well liked by all the other kids.

As the kids in the class began to pass out their gifts to one another, some of them started laughing, wondering who this funny looking, skinny little kid was. Also, as children often do, they laughed mockingly because I had no gift to give and I would not be receiving one.

Suddenly, Dwight stood up with his hands on his hips and with a strong loud voice said, "Listen everybody, Russell is my cousin and you'd better leave him alone." He then walked over to where I was sitting and handed me his gift. It was a red rubber ball. He continued to sit and talk with me until class was over.

After church he invited me to go home with him. I felt like I was in Disneyland or Lego land – of course at that time I didn't even know those places existed. Dwight had toys the like of which I had never seen. Some of the toys he introduced to me could even talk. He also had his own merry-go-round in the back yard. Over a period of time, Dwight and I became very close and it seemed we were destined for our lives to intertwine for many years to come. He would become more than a cousin to me – he would become a brother.

About two weeks after I went to live with Aunt Ruth and Uncle Ralph, I had a wonderful surprise waiting for me when I came home from school. Someone at Uncle Ralph's work place told him the Children's Protective Agency was going to pick up Gwen so he told Aunt Ruth to go get her and bring her home. I was so excited to see Gwen; I immediately began showing her all the new clothes and toys our new parents had bought me.

In time, Gwen and I would forge a relationship that was very special. We were both thankful we had escaped foster care and could enjoy living together as brother and sister with caring relatives who treated us with respect and kindness.

My little sister, Louise, was also rescued by none other than my Aunt Ruth's sister - a wonderful woman named Naomi. Although Louise and I didn't get to live in the same house, it comforted my heart to know she had a great home with a family who treated her like their very own daughter.

Chapter 3 – Bullies and Learning Issues

Even though I was now living in a nice home with wonderful adoptive parents, I was still a very pitiful looking little boy who didn't understand how to go about in society. True, I was being fed hearty food but it would take some time for me to regain my health – I was very scrawny and underweight. Due to my malnourished and socially dysfunctional state, I was a prime candidate for the heartless bullying and mocking attitude from many of my peers in school.

I was of an age to be in the fourth grade when I went to live with Uncle Ralph and Aunt Ruth. Although my academic abilities were certainly not up to par, it was decided by the school staff to have me continue along in the fourth grade. Looking back, I have often thought it might have been a better decision to place me in third grade or some special education class. The decision made by school staff to leave me mainstreamed would greatly contribute to major problems in my academic and social environment.

Gwen was twelve years old – three years older than me. She became my protector and bodyguard. On several occasions she would run the bullies away from me. I will never forget the day we were at the school bus stop when a bully began picking on me. Gwen hit him over the head with the back of her book and proceeded to run him down the street. No one ever bothered me at the bus stop again. Unfortunately, Gwen couldn't be with me 24 hours a day.

Eventually came the years of junior high which can be difficult enough for thriving students. My years at Divisadero

Junior High School in Visalia were two of the toughest and worst years of my life. I was still socially awkward and very lonely and scared. The effects of malnutrition continued to hold on – I was small for my age and had a spirit of timidity.

All the bullies had a field day with me. There was one bully I will never forget. I will call him Gary. He was about six feet tall and one of the biggest kids on campus. One day as I was leaving the class to go home, he grabbed the back of my collar and proceeded to drag me all the way across campus to the ball field, yelling for everyone to come and watch.

About 200 students followed us to the ball field and gathered around. He made me kneel down and then gave me an ultimatum to either kiss his shoes or eat some dirt. If I didn't comply, he said he would knock my head off. This went on for about 15 minutes as I knelt there in the dirt quaking in my shoes, with tears running down my face.

I was hoping and praying that someone would see what was happening and come to my rescue. Perhaps one of the teachers would notice the crowd and come to see what was going on. It was a fruitless hope – not one teacher showed up.

It crossed my mind to hit him in the groin area and once he was distracted, I would hit him again as hard and fast as I could before running away. Better sense prevailed since I was pretty certain that tactic would not be successful and he would chase me down and seriously injure me. Finally, I just hit my forehead on the top of his shoe, grabbed some dirt in my hand and threw it down. Then I jumped up and took off running and pushing my way through the crowd as everyone began whooping and yelling.

The next morning I told Aunt Ruth I was sick and I didn't go to school for three days. I did not relate the bullying incident to her – she never realized it was a common occurrence. During the three days I stayed home, I had a lot of time to mull over the incident with Gary and made a firm decision – *"NEVER AGAIN."*

In addition to my social issues, I had a learning disability which contributed to my academic failure. Through my 7th and 8th grade years, I flunked every subject in school. I had straight F's on every report card. Being unable to read or comprehend basic arithmetic such as multiplication, subtraction and division was very frustrating to say the least.

Aunt Ruth worked diligently to help me in my studies. There were many days she worked at her fruit packing job in Ivanhoe for 11 or 12 hours. After work, she would come home, cook dinner, clean up the kitchen, then spend time and effort helping me comprehend my homework. I often wondered why she didn't give up on me. I now realize she loved me too much to leave me in the state I was in if she could do something about it.

One day she went to my school to have a one on one conference with Mr. Strain, my core teacher. She asked what more she could do to help me raise my failing grades. His reply was, "There is nothing that can be done. Russell is just dumb." In the next moment his desk was cleared off with just one sweep of her arm. She never told me what happened or what was said. All I know is the following day I began to receive extra attention from Mr. Strain – he sat me on the front row and made more of an effort with me. I didn't enjoy the extra attention.

Although my grades were not good enough to graduate from the 8th grade, I was allowed to take the Constitution Test, which was a requirement for students to pass in order to graduate from the 8th to the 9th grade.

I was informed by my teacher that if I could pass the Constitution Test, I would then be allowed to graduate with my class. As I sat in the classroom to take the test, I could look out the window and see my classmates practicing for the graduation exercise that would take place that night. I immediately proceeded to take and fail the Constitution Test four times. Finally, the instructor gave me the answer sheet and allowed me to take the test one more time. To everyone's amazement I got 100% correct.

That night I showed up to graduate. Because I had been occupied taking tests, I was not available to practice for the graduation ceremony. Whoever was in charge of the ceremony placed me behind one of the more capable students and said, "Follow him and do what he does." I watched him very closely. When they called his name, he walked upon the stage and they handed him his diploma. He raised his arms in celebration and all his friends and family cheered.

When they called my name, I walked out on stage and they handed me my diploma. I raised my arms to celebrate but no one cheered. However, I did hear the applause of two proud parents and my supportive sister. I was one frightened little boy as my thoughts turned toward the end of summer and my future high school years.

Chapter 4 – Summer Miracle

Still struggling with mental, physical and social impairments, little was I to realize the amazing miracle I would receive during the summer between my 8th and 9th grade years.

By this time I had been living with Aunt Ruth and Uncle Ralph for several years and I now considered them my mother and father and referred to them as such. During the years I lived with them, they took Gwen and me to church on a regular basis where we learned about Jesus and his healing power.

The church we attended was a small country church in a little community called Cameron Creek near Visalia, California. We had church services on Sunday morning, Sunday evening, Tuesday evening, Thursday evening and Saturday evening. An understanding of how many services we attended each week might be helpful for the reader to understand my next statement: *Most of my time in church was spent sleeping on the pew and trying to figure out the best way to pay as little attention to what was going on as possible.* In other words, like most young people, I was rather bored during all these services.

However, one Sunday night the preacher really got my attention. His subject was about hell and he described it as though he had been born and raised there. I found myself entranced as his descriptive words painted a picture of how hot and miserable hell would be if one was unfortunate enough to experience the place. He certainly scared the hell out of me!

Then he said something that really captured my attention. He said, “If you do not receive Jesus in your heart, you will be going to hell when you die.”

Though I paid little attention in church, I had observed enough to know what to do next. So, when the preacher stopped preaching I went forward to pray. As I stood in front of the whole church I suddenly realized I did not know how to pray. So instead, I just cried for two hours – a response which was very acceptable to the congregation. Showing emotion didn’t trouble them and the people in our church probably figured this pitiful little fellow needed a good cry. As was their custom, they were glad to comfort me while I cried my heart out.

After a period of time, the congregation slowly departed until the only ones remaining were my mother and the pastor. By this time I was totally exhausted so I continued to lie on the floor for some time without moving. My mother then asked a question that would lead to a profound change in my life. She asked me, “Russell what do you want?"

Of course, I had been thinking about getting Jesus in my heart so I would not go to hell. However, I was expecting a miniature Jesus about three inches high to come running down the aisle and jump into my heart. So when she asked me that question I replied. "I want Jesus to come into my heart.”

She said, "Well take Him, Honey. Just let Him in.”

I replied, "Okay.”

Suddenly I felt a warm sensation. It began at the top of my head and slowly covered my whole body. Something very powerful began to happen and at that moment I received a miracle. Instantly, I noticed a type of awareness in my being – a clarity of something I had never felt or seen up to that point in time. It didn't take me long to realize what I experienced that night would result in some very remarkable changes in my life.

For example, academically, it was as though I had been given an IQ boost. In the next few days, I began to realize that reading and comprehension came easier to me – the difference was like night and day. Also, math – multiplication, division and simple algebra – were no longer such a puzzle.

Physically, I also had some remarkable benefits. My left ear completely opened up and I could hear clearly. All of this happened in one moment of time when Jesus came into my heart.

Apparently, there was another change – that was my ability to sing. Our church was known for many talented people who were very gifted in singing. They didn't use traditional hymns when they sang. Instead they sang new songs from Stamps-Baxter song books. Nearly all could read music and sing four part harmony. There were several singing groups in the church that sang quartet style. On the first Saturday night of each month, singing conventions were held and the church would be packed out with standing room only.

I always wanted to sing but I couldn't carry a tune in a bucket. As a matter of fact most of the other kids laughed at me and no one wanted to stand near me when the singing began. There was a lot of special singing by various groups during our church services and since it was a big part of our social life, I very much wanted to be involved.

About two weeks after I received my miracle, I told my mother that I wanted to sing a solo in church – I didn't think I would stand a chance of getting a group to sing with me. She stared at me for a few moments and then she said, "Okay, I'll ask the pastor." That night the pastor introduced me to come to the platform to sing my solo. As I began to sing, chins on many of the adults dropped and the teenagers quit throwing spit wads as they paused to listen with surprised looks on their faces. I'll never forget the name of the song.

I chose the song written by Stuart Hamblen – "How Big is God."[1] The words are as follows:

Verse 1
Tho' man may strive to go beyond the reach of space
To crawl beyond the distant shining stars
This world's a room so small within my Master's house
The open sky but a portion of his yard

Chorus
How big is God? How big and wide his vast domain
To try to tell, these lips could only start
He's big enough to rule His mighty universe
Yet small enough to live within my heart

Verse 2
As winter chill may cause the tiny seed to fall
To lie asleep 'til waked by summer's rain
The heart grown cold will warm and rock with life anew
The Master's touch will bring the glow again

I was singing in front of the same people who had heard about the miracle I received two weeks earlier. Now, they're hearing me sing about the Man who lives within my heart. At the end of the song, some of them were crying and some were laughing – all were rejoicing. That was the beginning of a singing ministry that would become a very enjoyable part of my life.

Along with continuing to sing solos, I was soon invited to be in trios, quartets, ensembles and choirs. I was also regularly assigned to lead the congregation during our church song service. In those days, we didn't refer to the congregational singing as "worship service" – it was simply "song service."

Uncle Ralph and Aunt Ruth owned the house we lived in. It was located in a small three street subdivision in Cameron Creek about seven miles east of Visalia, California. All of the houses were built during the 1930's and 1940's and were made of single boards without insulation. Some of them had no inside toilets, including ours, until we build a new house on the same location in 1961.

Four houses down the street was another family – the Taff Family. Joe and Ann Taff had five boys and we regularly played together even though we would have our occasional rock fight. We all became very good friends and attended the same church until their father became the pastor of another local church.

The Taff family was well known because they were very good singers and musicians. One of the sons, Russ Taff, became internationally known as a singer with The Imperials and as a solo artist, winning several Grammys and other music awards. He also became a member of the Gaither Vocal Band and has toured with Bill Gaither in the Gaither Homecoming Concerts. One of his best known singing performances is of the song "Praise the Lord."

My cousin, Dwight, was also a very gifted singer and piano player. He was highly sought out for these excellent skills to either participate in or lead various groups including choirs. He had an amazing first tenor voice. In later years he would travel and sing with various groups including The Songfellows.

I continue to have a great appreciation for my Christian heritage and all that it entailed including the wonderful music we enjoyed during those years.

Chapter 5 – A New Boy Enters High School

In September of 1959, about one month after the miracle in my life, I was scheduled to begin my 9th grade year at Mt. Whitney High School in Visalia. I would turn 14 years old on September 18 and little did I know the direction my life was soon to take. In fact, the transformation in my life was so profound, my former classmates from junior high hardly recognized me. My countenance had changed – the spirit of timidity which had ruled my life for so long was now lifted and my new confidence was apparent for all to see.

I especially noticed the bullies and people who formerly mocked and made fun of me had ceased that kind of activity with one exception. His name was Corky. One day during my first semester in high school, Corky began bullying a kid who was intellectually challenged. There were about 30 of us standing around the exit door of woodshop waiting for the bell to ring so we could head out to our next class. Finally, the kid who was being bullied began to cry but Corky would not let up.

I decided I couldn’t take it any longer so I walked over and said, "Corky, why don't you pick on somebody your own size?" Then, I knew I was in trouble.

He said, "OK, I'll just pick on you.” Corky then began mocking me and pushing me across the large woodshop. Finally he had me up against the drill press and there was no place for me to turn. My arms were loaded with school books and I felt very defenseless. The same fear I had experienced in previous times began to come over me.

Then I remembered the vow I had made to myself after what I experienced with Gary, *"NEVER AGAIN!!"* It's hard to explain it went so fast. I suddenly dropped my books, my left fist hit him in the stomach and I delivered a right cross and hit him beside the nose just below his left eye and – you got it – *"Down goes Corky!! Down goes Corky!!"*

He lay on the floor knocked out cold. His four bully friends looked at me in shock and then after what seemed like five minutes, picked him up and carried him across campus to the nurse's office.

Because we were between classes, many students saw his friends carrying him and asked what happened. One of his friends spoke up and said, "He was picking on Russell McCollough and Russell knocked him out." Corky didn't come back to school for three days. His buddies reported his nose broken and his left eye swollen shut. Amazingly, no one ever mocked or bullied me again. Unlike the time Gary bullied me, this time I did not tell Aunt Ruth I was sick nor did I spend three days at home. Although I didn't feel pleased with myself for the damage I inflicted upon Corky, it was some consolation to realize I had overcome enough of my old fear of being bullied to stick up for a person who couldn't stick up for himself.

Later in the school year, I started being friendly toward Corky and we became good friends. To my knowledge he never mocked or bullied anyone again.

Even though I had failed physical education in the 7th and 8th grades, I soon discovered I loved to run. The miracle I experienced had transformed me physically to the point that I could run far and I could run fast. Forest Gump had nothing on me.

Because of my speed all the coaches wanted me to come out on their teams, especially the football coach. My mother said *"No"* to the football team, however, she allowed me to participate in track.

I loved to run the mile and in my Senior year - 1963, I completed the mile in less than four minutes and thirty seconds. That time is considered to be a very fast time for high school even today.

Chapter 6 – Trip to Texas

In the summer of 1960 between my 9th and 10th grade years, my cousin Dwight graduated from high school and his parents purchased him a new Oldsmobile Cutlass for his graduation gift.

Our parents agreed that we could travel together in his new car to Dallas, Texas where we would attend two weeks of musical training at the Stamps-Baxter School of Music. During our time there, we were hosted by a wonderful Christian family.

While in Dallas, one night I began I began to experience the old earache again. I had not experienced an earache since receiving my miracle one year earlier. The infection caused the fever in my body to begin rising to the point that I was no longer aware of what I was doing or saying. Dwight and I were the only ones at home as our hosts had gone out for the evening. Needless to say, my actions and nonsensical conversation really freaked Dwight out.

I have no personal recollection of anything I said or did during this time. However, over the years Dwight has been faithful to fill me in with all the details. As I was talking nonsense, he was calling out to God for help and in between his prayers kept asking me, "Rusty what's wrong? What's wrong with you? What are you doing?"

Apparently I was pacing through the house as Dwight followed me around asking, "What can I do for you? Do you want a glass of water? Do you want a banana?"

Later, he told me I said, "No I don't want a banana but I'll take a glass of water."

He related to me that I took one sip of water and then turned the glass upside down on the table spilling water everywhere. He asked me again, "What is the matter?"

I replied, "I don't know. It must be that banana I ate." But, of course I hadn't eaten the banana – I was simply out of my mind with fever.

After about two hours my ear quit aching, the fever subsided and I finally came to myself. We shared the same bedroom but Dwight got very little sleep probably feeling he didn't dare take his eyes off me the rest of the night.

A few days later the music school ended and we left Texas to travel back to California. As we were going over the Tehachapi Mountains, the elevation caused my ear to become irritated and as it began to ache, my temperature climbed again. Through the pain and fever, I was aware of Dwight praying loudly calling upon God to help me. We were about two hours from home and he was exceeding the speed limit in his attempt to get me home as soon as possible. I'm sure he felt helpless to do anything for me and wanted to get me in the hands of my parents.

As soon as we got home, Dwight ran into the house to get my mother and explained as best as he could what had transpired with me. They helped me out of the car into the house and laid me on the couch. For the next four hours I was unaware of where I was, what I was doing and what I was saying. It was not uncommon for my parents to call the church family for prayer instead of rushing to the doctor and this time wouldn't be an exception.

My mother called a few people from the church to come and help her pray. Now these people were very earnest and fervent in their prayer. They were determined not to give up until I had some relief. Suddenly, I came into consciousness and woke up in a cold sweat. The fever had broken and my ear was no longer aching.

I have not had another earache with accompanying high fever since that night. Over the years I have had several hearing tests. The doctors would always comment about a lot of scarring in my left ear but the hearing in my left ear was always as good as the hearing in my right ear. I began to realize more than ever God was making an investment in my life and perhaps there was a purpose for me which would be further revealed in the fullness of time.

Chapter 7 – I Meet my Future Wife

In 1966, a very special family began attending Cameron Creek Church – the Tabor Family. Owen and Bessie Tabor had eight children – one son and seven daughters. The older three – Betty, Cletus and Owen Jr. were married with families of their own.

Of the daughters remaining at home, there was Cherry, Judy, Sandra, Connie, and Brenda. *Judy is the one that got my attention.* She would later let me know that although she definitely wanted my attention, she wasn't aware that her feelings were reciprocated. I was 21 and Judy was 17.

The Tabor family had been attending Cameron Creek Church off and on for approximately one year. Due to the fact that they lived some distance from the church they often attended a church closer to their home and were not regular in their attendance at Cameron Creek.

During the time they attended Cameron Creek, Judy dated a few boys in the church – none seriously – just friendship dating. I was interested in her but I wasn't sure if she was serious about these guys she was dating.

One Sunday I made up my mind that if the Tabor family attended church that evening I would ask Judy if I could take her home even though they lived 30 miles away.

Sure enough, while I was leading the song service that night I noticed Judy was indeed in the audience. As soon as the song service portion of church was over I left on a quick errand.

Gwen was now married to a great guy named Ford Tucker. They lived a short distance from the church and had recently purchased a new black Dodge Dart. Although I had a 1954 Chevy, I felt the need to impress Judy by borrowing their new car to drive her home in – that is, if she was kind enough to accept my invitation.

Ford was generous enough to loan me his car and handed me the keys. When I finally got back to the church, the sanctuary was full and there was only one seat left which happened to be right by Judy.

Although I was quaking in my shoes, I got my nerve up and sat down beside her. It must have been a God thing. I didn't find out until later that sitting behind us was another young man who had already asked Judy if he could take her home. Judy had declined hoping this might be the night I would pick up enough courage to ask her out. Right on!!

That particular evening the speaker was a visiting missionary who had traveled to exotic locations. He had a display at the front of the church with some snake and alligator skins which he put out for viewing. When church was over I asked Judy if she would like to go with me to look at the display. I was attempting to extend our time together in order to get up the nerve to ask if I could take her home. She was very cooperative and stood there with me as we studied those snake and alligator skins. Finally, I ran out of time so I popped the question, inquiring if I could take her home. She said, "Sure, I'll let my parents know you'll be driving me home."

Well, she stole my heart that night and it was the beginning of many, many 60 mile round-trips with no regrets just to date her.

Chapter 8 – Army Life

As I mentioned previously, I had been very successful in track during my high school years. I was honored with All American status and offered various track scholarships. When I left high school, I had made the honor roll every semester and graduated with a 3.50 GPA. The young man who couldn't pass the Constitution Test without the answer sheet had come a long way.

Since I didn't want to venture too far from home, I decided it would be best to attend College of the Sequoias (COS) – a junior college close to home in Visalia.

After attending COS for two years, I accepted a track scholarship from Fresno State College – later to be re-named Fresno State University. In college my primary event became the quarter mile (440 yard dash). In my last year of college my best times in this event were under 47 seconds. I had aspirations to try out for the 1968 Olympic Team in Mexico City.

However, undeclared war was raging in Viet Nam and we also had the North-South Korean Conflict going on so the U.S. had troops stationed in South Korea. It seemed as though Uncle Sam had different plans for me than something as enjoyable as making my bid for the Olympics. I received my draft notice and I was one unhappy young man.

After being inducted in Seattle, Washington, I was flown to San Antonio, Texas where I was trained at Fort Sam Houston to be a medical corpsman. This was a very disrupting time in my young adult life. I had been courting Judy for a year and as a young man head over heels in love; I did not want to go into the army. This was during the height of the Vietnam conflict, I therefore concluded in my mind that's where I would be headed after basic and medical corpsman training.

Following the six months of training at Fort Sam Houston, I came home on leave and Judy and I were married on December 23, 1967 in Cameron Creek Church with more than 250 family members and friends in attendance. We had a wonderful two weeks together and then I was flown – not to Vietnam where there was such a high demand for medics – but to South Korea. Needless to say, that was a very welcome relief.

After arriving in Seoul, Korea, I was shipped about 35 miles north to the border that separates North Korea from South Korea. The army camp I was stationed at was Camp Casey. As the head company medic, I was given a medical jeep to drive and every night I would follow the trucks of troops up to the front lines where we would bunker down in foxholes to guard against any infiltration from the North Koreans.

The buffer zone that separated North Korea from South Korea was called the Demilitarized Zone (DMZ) which was approximately one mile wide. However, there was nothing demilitarized about it. Every day we would send a patrol of 12 armed soldiers into the zone to look for threatening activities from the North Koreans.

Of course the North Koreans were sending their soldiers into the zone as well. One day there was a conflict I will never forget. We received a radio message from one of our patrols stating they had been ambushed by a North Korean company of soldiers. We lost radio contact only to find out later their radio had been shot and was out of order.

Before we lost contact, we were able to ascertain they needed a medic and of course that was me. We put together another patrol and we headed into the zone looking for the patrol that had been ambushed. Due to the fact we had lost contact, we had no idea where they were so we wandered around looking for them. Wow, did we feel vulnerable!

As we were wandering around we had to wade through a little creek. Continuing on for the next 30 minutes we suddenly heard troops behind us yelling for us to get down. When we turned around and looked at them they were frantically waving their arms. We knew these were the troops we were looking for but we had no idea why they were acting in the manner they were. Suddenly, we realized we had gone too far and that we were now in North Korea.

The thought registered rather forcefully we must immediately get out of that area or we would be captured or shot. We turned around and started running south toward the group that was waving at us. We had no choice but to run up the side of a mountain with our backs to North Korea.

When we got to the patrol we were looking for, they grabbed us, threw us down behind some cover and said, "Are you guys crazy? Look behind you." We turned and looked. About 200 yards behind us were approximately 100 North Korean soldiers on the top of the ridge with their rifles trained on us. It was apparent they were having problems with their weapons because they would not fire.

They would put their rifles in the firing position, lower them, pause and look at them and then pound on them. Finally, the North Koreans ran back in the direction they came from. I immediately began giving medical aid to four wounded men. Unfortunately, there was a casualty to this conflict – we carried out one dead soldier who was killed when the first patrol was ambushed. Three other soldiers had minor gunshot wounds.

I knew this incident would cause worry back home if it was ever recorded or broadcast in the media. This was right after the infamous "Pueblo Incident" and things were very heated up between the U.S. and North Korea.

As I was writing home to explain to my mother and Judy what happened, my mother was also writing a letter to me. She had dreamed that night I was in danger. She said she saw me wading through a little creek of water. She immediately got up and began to pray. Our letters must have crossed paths in the mail. By the time she received the letter I had written to her, I had also received the letter she had written to me about her dream.

I had a new Super 8 movie camera and took a lot of movies as a remembrance of my time while in Korea. A few days after the rescue of the troops, I took my camera back to the area of the creek our patrol had waded through on our way to get to the troops and filmed the creek and surrounding area.

When I came home and showed the movies to my family, at one point my mother asked me to pause and back up the film. When I came to the place that showed the scene of the creek, she asked me to stop the movie. She then said that was the creek she saw in her dream. I became more and more convinced God had his hand upon me and a definite purpose for my life.

When my time in Korea was completed in March 1969, I was discharged from the army and returned to my wonderful wife, Judy. Together we would find God's purpose for our lives..

Chapter 9 – Marriage and Family

Upon my return from the army, Judy and I settled down together in Porterville where she had been working since we were married. She was the secretary at Rehab Services at Porterville State Hospital. With her contacts, she managed to have a job waiting on me at the hospital's school. Although it was a temporary job, it provided me with a good transition from army to civilian life.

We lived in Porterville until the fall of 1969 when I received a call from Dwight asking us to consider moving to Roseville, California where he and his family were now located. He and some friends had formed a gospel quartet and he wanted me to come and be a part of the group.

The name of the quartet was the "Gospel Jubilee Quartet." The members of this group would work during the week at their regular jobs and then on a couple of Sundays each month, would travel to area churches and perform concerts. The musical style was country gospel similar to The Gaithers.

Judy and I looked forward with great anticipation to our new life in Roseville. Once we settled in we began attending our new church – Roseville Gospel Tabernacle. This was the church Dwight and his lovely wife, Kay, attended, along with their two young children, Keith and Diana. Our pastors were John and Madelon Opperman and they, along with the congregation, made us feel very welcome.

Before long we were very involved in the life of the church. I continued to travel with the quartet to other area churches so

I missed a couple of Sunday services each month but we tried to be as faithful as possible to the church services and other activities. Dwight directed the church choir and Judy and I both sang in the choir. I played on the men's fast pitch softball team and Judy was the team's scorekeeper. We loved our new friends and our church.

Judy worked for the State of California in downtown Sacramento and I began to work for Retail Credit Company (now known as Equifax) as an insurance investigator. We lived in an apartment in Citrus Heights – an unincorporated town near Roseville. Dwight and Kay also lived in Citrus Heights and we were able to visit with them on a regular basis.

Then, Judy and I took a big step and purchased our first home in Citrus Heights. On September 30, 1970 we welcomed our first baby – a daughter, Christa Lynn. We also purchased a beautiful new 1970 blue Dodge Charger. Life was good. I was making a good salary and Judy was able to quit working and stay home with our baby.

We then made a decision based on emotion that would get us off track for several years. Early in 1971, I left my job; we found renters for our home and we moved back to the Visalia area.

My parents were happy with our decision to move back and it was great to be living near them and Gwen and Ford. Although we loved our church at Cameron Creek and they welcomed us back, something about our return didn't feel exactly right and we struggled financially. In later years, I would come to realize that we were not in the place we were destined to be with our lives. In truth, we had most likely made a pretty major mistake when we moved from Roseville back to Visalia.

The absolute best thing that happened during this time was the birth of another lovely little daughter. On November 30, 1971, Angela Dawn was born – 14 months to the day after Christa's birth.

After months of struggling financially, eventually I went to work for Prudential Insurance. It turned out to be a good career choice for me and I greatly enjoyed working with my new manager, Reed Pepper. He was a Christian and God blessed me in my business.

Chapter 10 – God Gives Us a "Do-Over"

In August of 1975, it was as though we were allowed a "do over." Once again I received a call from Dwight. He said he had a job for me working as a Sales Representative for Nestle Chocolate if I wanted to take it. We barely had to think about whether or not to move back to the Roseville area. The answer was a resounding – "YES!"

We had purchased a little house in the community of Farmersville and immediately put it up for sale as we quickly prepared to move back to the Sacramento-Roseville area. Our friends at our former church in Roseville, including the Oppermans, welcomed us once again with open hearts.

One of the families in the church would be traveling on vacation for a month and they offered to make their home available for us to live in while they were gone. We were well pleased to take them up on their generous offer. This enabled us to have a place to live while we got settled in and found a home. School would begin in a few weeks and it would be time for Christa to enter Kindergarten.

Once the sale of our home in Farmersville was realized, we purchased a home in the Foothill Farms area and enrolled Christa in Kindergarten. Christa would turn 5 in just a few weeks. By this time, Angela had outgrown Christa and the Kindergarten teacher motioned for her to come into the class thinking she was also a Kindergartener. Judy explained to the teacher that Angela was only 3 years old and would not be enrolled in Kindergarten for another year.

I settled in at the Nestle Company and worked there for a few years. Eventually, Dwight and Kay and their family moved back to the Visalia area to help his parents on the farm where he had grown up.

We missed Dwight and Kay and their family but Judy and I were pleased to remain right where we were. Our little family had become very entrenched in our church and we had many friends. We especially loved our pastors and tried to help in whatever way we could. We served as youth pastors and I continued to be involved in the music ministry and served as Secretary of the Church Board of Directors.

By this time, I had decided to leave Nestle's and go back to work for Prudential Insurance in their Sacramento Office. Again, this was a good choice – with deregulation, the insurance business was thriving. I never had another manager quite like Reed Pepper, however, and I missed him a lot.

Then in 1977, some things began to happen that would have a big effect on the direction of our lives. Our current pastors, the Oppermans, decided it was time to retire.

Although we were sorry to see them go, our congregation's choice in our new pastors was very exciting and we welcomed them with open hearts. They were a young couple with two children who had previously traveled as evangelists.

Chapter 11 – Stepping into Our Destiny

We continued to serve our new pastors and our church – myself as trustee and youth pastor and then I was asked by our pastor to become the Minister of Music. We had a talented group of singers and I greatly enjoyed the times we had together.

But, after two short years – in 1979, some circumstances contributed to misunderstandings and confusion within our church. Our young pastor decided that he would resign the church and leave the area.

Many in the church were somewhat discouraged in the midst of the confusion including Judy and me. The church congregation found themselves in a difficult situation. We loved our pastors and grieved to see their family leave.

It seemed we would have no choice but to seek out another pastor to lead us. I was one of three men chosen from the church trustees selected to a "pulpit committee." It would be our job to try to find suitable candidates for the position of pastor.

There were three or four preachers in the region that made themselves available for candidates. However, there wasn't a consensus among the pulpit committee regarding which candidate to put before the trustees and the congregation for a confirming vote.

Even though Judy and I had been very happy at our church, in my heart I had always longed to travel as an evangelist and minister by singing and speaking in churches across the

United States. Needless to say, Judy was not enthusiastic about selling out and traveling across the United States in a motor home with two little girls. But it was always there in the back of my mind.

During this time of turmoil in our church, the thoughts of this type of traveling ministry became more prominently fixed in my mind.

In the meantime, here I am serving on a pulpit committee to help find a pastor for a church that I no longer want to be a part of. To me, the thought of traveling was looking better and better.

A couple of weeks went by and it seemed the pulpit committee was making very little progress. In frustration, I decided I would resign from the pulpit committee, sell our house, quit my secular job, buy a motor home and begin itinerating as an evangelist. I must have been hallucinating at the time but, I just wanted out of the situation I found myself in.

Our pastor had not yet left us so I thought I would go to his home and attempt to explain to him how much the people loved his family and that he should not resign. He received me well, however, he wanted no part of my ideas and although he didn't realize it, I left his house in tears.

The next thing I knew I was on a RV sales lot. As I walked through one motor home and then another, I noticed there were no sales reps following me around. I soon found out why. At one point, while standing in one of the motor homes, I heard the Lord speak to my spirit and say, *"What about my people in Roseville?"* I immediately broke down and started sobbing uncontrollably. I knew at that moment God was calling me to be the pastor of our church.

I began to make excuses by telling the Lord that I had never done that before. I had only preached about ten sermons to any general assembly in my whole life. I was 33 years old at the time and although I had served as a youth pastor, a trustee, Sunday school teacher and choir director, I just did not feel I was qualified to pastor. Yet in my heart of hearts, I knew it was a done deal.

Suddenly, I realized I had a problem – I was still on the pulpit committee. How would I tell the committee that I am putting myself forth to be considered a candidate for pastor? Before I acted, I decided to contact one of my close friends who was also on the pulpit committee in order to get some counsel. But first I needed to speak with Judy.

I left the RV sales lot and went home. There I spoke with Judy and told her what I had been thinking. Now, you must realize that in Judy's mind, she never had any dreams of being in the ministry except as we had previously been serving in lay ministry roles. The position of my serving full time as the lead pastor of a church – any church - was, to say the least, not her idea of how she wanted to spend her life.

Although I wasn't fully aware of it at the time, some of Judy's thoughts were based on her preconceived ideas of what she thought about the role of a pastor's wife and all that it entailed. In short, she didn't feel qualified in any way, shape, form or fashion.

Judy was well versed in the scripture and had a very solid foundation being raised in church all of her life. As opposed to many young people growing up in church, Judy actually listened to the preaching and teaching during those years.

Somehow she couldn't quite picture herself in the role of what she pictured as a proper pastor's wife which was basically an ultra sober-minded, *watch-what-you-say-and-do-all-the-time* type of person.

Thankfully, she didn't voice any negative thoughts regarding what I felt God was speaking to me. Typically, she would have no problem speaking exactly what was on her mind so I appreciated the fact that she didn't discourage me or make light of what I felt God was speaking. There was one major thing we had working in our favor – both of us had always nurtured a strong desire to do whatever God was calling us to do. We felt a great sense of destiny and purpose. Later, she would tell me that she thought, *"Well, we shall see where this will lead."*

My next step was to call my friend and tell him I needed to talk to him. He said, "Okay let's meet, I need to talk with you also."

When we got together, I immediately asked the question, "What do you want to talk to me about?"

He answered, "No, first of all I want to hear what you have to say."

I then told him about my experience on the RV sales lot and that God was calling me to pastor the church. I'll never forget that moment. He took a deep breath and his eyes got really big. I thought, *"Wow! Is he ever going to chew me out for adding further complications to our task!"*

Then he said, "That is exactly what I want to talk to you about. Never in my life have I used the phrase, *'God spoke to me or God said'* but I'm saying it now – God told me you are the man. *God wants you to be the next pastor*."

I told him I would not promote myself or campaign in any way and that if I were to be the candidate chosen to be put before the people, he was to inform the rest of the pulpit committee without my presence. In this way they would be free to share their own opinions regarding my qualifications and candidacy.

While my friend and I were speaking together, Judy was at home walking the floors praying and seeking God. She later told me she felt God speaking into her spirit for what seemed like hours, giving her scriptures and confirming what was to be. In those days we knew very little about the prophetic but in later years, the specific things that came to Judy during that time would be proven over and over again.

After my friend went to speak to the pulpit committee and the trustees, they all agreed to present me as the candidate to be recommended to the church for pastor. Two weeks later I was confirmed as the new pastor of the church.

My first Sunday as pastor, we had a full house. My message was titled, *"I have never done this before."* I used examples from the Bible like the man who was laid at the gate called Beautiful who had never walked before, Moses who had never opened the Red Sea before and Joshua who had never marched around the walls of Jericho before."

Truthfully, I was impressed with myself so I was looking forward to the next Sunday with great expectancy hoping for an even larger crowd. When the day finally arrived, 30% of the congregation didn't show up. I had heard of "Exodus Revivals" but this was my first.

Actually, we were aware that a few of the people desired a different candidate to be put before the church so we weren't surprised when some folks left. We had steadfast hearts and knew beyond a shadow of any doubt that God had set us in. We would need this childlike confidence in the days ahead

Chapter 12 – Pastoring-Early Years

During my first few months of serving as pastor at Roseville Gospel Tabernacle, as inexperienced as I was and although Judy and I came into the pastorate during difficult days, the grace of God was with us. It helped that people were very supportive, kind and patient.

However, as the months went by, I found that, "on the job training", was very difficult. Although I kept it to myself, many Sundays following the morning service, as I drove home with a heavy heart, I would plead with God saying, "I can't do this – I don't know what to do."

Actually, every Sunday I would tell God I was quitting. Still running through my mind was the idea of leaving it all and hitting the road and trying out the idea of evangelizing. The thoughts of the motor home scenario were never very far from my mind and it would have been easy to have forgotten about *"God's people in Roseville."* Of course, I didn't dare bring this up to Judy because she had never warmed to the motor home idea in the first place.

There was one Sunday I will never forget. As I was driving home in tears I told God once again, "I quit!"

He said, "Why don't you let me build my church?" I remember thinking, *"Good idea – after all, it is your Church."*

A few weeks later, I was attending a church growth conference in Lamont, California, a small town on the outskirts of Bakersfield. Pastor Kemp Holden, of Harvest

Time Tabernacle in Fort Smith, Arkansas was teaching one of the sessions.

The principles and concepts he was sharing on leadership really grabbed my attention. I will never forget a question he asked us. He said, "Have you ever seen a church that has lost its morale?"

I thought to myself, *"Have I ever seen one? I am pastoring one."*

He then said, "That is the reflection of the pastor's vision." I immediately ducked my head behind the pew in front of me and began to weep. I realized that changes were needed and I knew when I returned to my church I would be a man with a new mission.

I began increasing my prayer time and took a new look at the Bible, the blessed Word of God, as though I had never seen it before. This became a very refreshing approach. Instead of studying the Bible in order to develop a message for the church, I began to see what God was saying to me in a personal way. This caused my relationship with God to become more intimate. It was out of those experiences that I began to share from my heart, fresh messages to the church, and we began connecting in a new way.

Not only did my vision for the house and for the community become clearer but I began to see that we needed to make some changes in our church services. We took the hymnals out of the church and began to lead the congregation in contemporary songs. I began to teach and demonstrate to the church a new style of worship patterned after what Judy and I had heard coming out of Bible Temple in Portland, Oregon where Dick Iverson pastored.

In addition I began teaching about faith principles and the truth that there is nothing impossible with God. An excitement came upon the church as we entered into a time of experiencing miracles, deliverances and new births into the Kingdom of God.

Over the course of time we also incorporated some major changes in our Christian Education Ministry. We decided to discontinue our Sunday morning Sunday school. This enabled us to have a full worship service in the main sanctuary while our children were having children's church with ministry more suited to their age group(s).

Our service began to include praise and worship utilizing dynamic, uplifting songs and sermons focused on encouragement and meeting the needs of the people. What was formerly known as Sunday school was moved to a midweek service. We eventually changed the name of our church from Roseville Gospel Tabernacle to Living Water Community Church in an effort to better reflect our vision and our mission. Not all of these changes were favorable to everyone but we pressed on.

During these years, Judy and I were spending a lot of time building into our little family. Through the years, we had witnessed the heartache many pastors suffered as they built a great church but saw their own children not only leave the church but also leave the Faith of their parents.

We counted ourselves fortunate to be able to sit under great teaching from Pastors Kemp and Carol Holden and Pastors Charles and Barbara Green regarding the family life of those in ministry.

This teaching freed us to be comfortable placing our children in the priority they deserved. We endeavored to use the following basic model of the desired relationship priorities for our lives:

1) Jesus
2) Family
3) Ministry

Judy and I decided we would do everything possible to avoid undue expectations being placed upon our daughters by the members of the congregation. If any expectations were to be placed upon them, they would be placed by us. Our children were not in the ministry in those days – they were simply– our little girls. We had a meeting with Christa and Angela and said we had always expected them to obey and being pastors of the church wouldn't change anything. We would continue to require a high standard of obedience, not because we were pastors, rather because they were our children and nothing was changing in that regard.

Of course, there were many seasons when it seemed as if we were putting the church first, but when taken as a whole, Christa and Angela were the sunshine of our lives and we loved spending time and having fun together as a family. We involved them in as many aspects of church life as possible.

Christa was 8 and Angela was 7 when we began pastoring. Each Sunday, it was their job to place the bulletins in straight formation behind the pews. Never have I seen two little girls who loved the church activities and church family more than these two. Moreover, the church family loved them and treated them like the little princesses they were.

Although we had very little in the way of money, we managed to put Christa and Angela in a lot of activities through our community recreation center. Of primary importance to us was exposing them to as many types of activities as possible so they could make a quality choice in their decision to pursue at least one primary activity. Once they decided what those might be, we would make the effort to obtain private lessons or whatever it took to give them the opportunity to further develop their skills.

Christa ultimately chose music and Angela chose swimming. Through Christa's young life, she played the bass guitar, violin and piano. In addition, she developed her voice in private and public – taking voice lessons and singing in groups, directing choirs, leading worship and singing solos. At the age of 15, she was placed on the schedule to lead our church congregation in worship.

Both girls swam on recreation swim teams from the time they were 6 and 7 years old until their teen years. During the summer months, Judy and I would load everyone up and go to the Saturday morning swim meets. I was usually a timer and Judy was in charge of the "ready" bench. Christa and Angie sat under tented areas with their swim mates having the time of their lives in between swimming events.

Being a competitive family, when it came time for their races, we were front and center to see if they would improve their times. Those were some of the most fun and memorable days of our lives together as a family. At the end of the season, we would meet at Sierra College in Rocklin for Championships along with all the teams we swam against during the year.

It was always our desire to place Christa and Angela in a Christian School once they left elementary school. However, since both girls required braces, we could not afford a private school – it would have to be a public education for both girls.

We would debrief them on a regular basis when they came home from school. It was a great blessing to see how God used their lives as a witness to many of their classmates over the years.

During their pre-teen years, we explained to them that some of their friends would ultimately choose a lifestyle that would preclude Christa and Angela from spending a lot of time with them. But, we further explained they would *never* lack for "fun" stuff to do.

When those days came, it was very difficult for both girls – especially Christa who was more into the social life of school. Angela was well liked and had a lot of friends but by this time she was swimming year round which meant she was spending six hours each day either swimming or traveling to and from the pool which left little time for a social life.

That period in life became very difficult as so many of their school mates moved in a different direction than Christa and Angela in a season of partying, drinking alcohol and sexual activity. But, true to our word, we tried to fill in with good times – inviting their friends to our home, taking them to Christian concerts, joining up with other youth group activities. Whatever it took – we determined they would have a full, rich life.

Both girls continued to have favor with their classmates throughout their school years. Christa was the Junior Prom Queen, the Senior Ball Queen and was voted by her graduating class to receive the Senior Class Citizenship Award. Angela lettered four years on the Varsity Swim Team and was President of her Senior Class. Both girls attended Portland Bible College and later Angela attended Sierra College in Rocklin.

During their young adult years, both girls traveled on missions trips – Christa to Russia, Albania and Romania and Angela to Mexico and China.

I want to give credit for the wonderful family members and friends who supported us along the way by taking a huge interest in the lives of our daughters. Our friend, Donna Bailey, was like an older sister and part time mother to Christa and Angela. Our girls never lacked for familial support whether it came through actual family members such as aunts and uncles or church family members who served as aunts, uncles, cousins – whatever the need was, they didn't lack for support and love.

If there is one thing Judy and I can say of a certainty, our daughters were always a high priority in our lives and as we look back upon their growing up years, we have only fond memories of our time and life together. They were more than daughters; they became our friends and companions.

Chapter 13 – Arise and Build

As mentioned previously, we began to make changes in the way we conducted our church services. In fact, we were one of many churches across the country in the process of such transitions. We didn't make changes for change sake; rather we believed God was the initiator of the progression His church was taking.

Within a few years, our Sunday morning services were full and on occasion, we had standing room only. Expansion seemed to be the logical decision. A temporary solution was to make a small addition to our existing building which gave us a little extra room – we added enough space for two offices and built larger bathrooms. Then, when a small building next door to the church became available, we rented it and this gave us room for two small offices and two additional classrooms.

A major problem was our lack of a church owned parking lot. Our current building was located in downtown Roseville and included only ten parking spaces. This left our congregation with the option of finding parking on the street or in the parking lot belonging to an auto parts store which was thankfully, closed on Sundays. We were landlocked on all sides and as our church grew the need for additional parking grew.

Then, one day we learned Roseville Telephone Company was building a very nice parking lot on some land to the right of our church. Since they had only a skeleton staff on the weekends, it was as though we had our very own new parking lot. We filled it up every Sunday. Later a local bank built another parking lot on the other side of the church so we also had that space available to us on the weekends. This made three parking lots directly adjacent to the church which served us well unless we had a function during a weekday – then people had to park and walk from wherever they could find a space.

Partly because we were in the process of continuing to introduce new methods of "having church" to the congregation, it became apparent that it might be good for our church to host an annual Bible Conference once each year. Although Judy and I and some of our leaders traveled to conferences in different parts of the U.S. where we had the opportunity to receive teaching and ministry from a variety of ministries, this type of travel wasn't feasible for the vast majority of our congregation.

40 years ago, people didn't have the media choices available today. Yes, there were tape cassettes, books and televangelists but some of the ministries we wanted to expose our congregation to didn't have national television programs. However, they were very successful pastors in their own areas. We had a strong desire to expose our congregation to some of these pastors and their ministries.

It was evident to me that if our people could hear what we were hearing, it would be easier for them to come on board and catch the vision with some of the changes I believed God wanted us to make. Thus, the idea of hosting an annual conference at our church would allow us to bring in quality speakers and ministries for a few days and nights each year. This would give our church exposure to the ministries we so admired and looked up to as examples of what we had aspirations to and what we wanted our own ministry and church to resemble.

We knew that God had a unique plan for us but it never hurts to have examples of what success looks like. Flash and sparkle wasn't what we looked for – seasoned tried and true ministries were the types we wanted to bring in for our conference.

We were very excited about this new endeavor as we entered into the preparations for our first conference. After meeting Pastor Kemp Holden at Lamont, we decided to ask him to be our first conference speaker.

In fact, over the years, he became one of our favorite conference speakers and we invited him to come and speak several times. He was a tremendous blessing to Judy and me as well as to the congregation.

It was through Pastor Holden that we first met Pastor Charles Green from New Orleans, Louisiana. As soon as we heard him speak, we knew we wanted him to come and be our main speaker at our conference the following year. At the time, we had no idea of the influence he would have over our church family and some major decisions we would make that would affect the future of the church.

So it was that we invited Pastor Charles Green to come to our 1986 church conference to be our main speaker during the four day conference. He had become one of our favorite speakers over the years – his messages were timely, inspirational and full of humor and wisdom.

He was scheduled to speak several times at the conference. Although his sermons during the conference were well received, I did not feel the connection with his messages as it related to our church and our situation. On the last day of the conference, we went out for lunch and I said, "Pastor Green I have heard you many times and you were always very dynamic but I just feel like something is missing or perhaps it's just me and I'm not connecting."

I'll never forget his response. He answered, "Don't say another word. What is going to happen tonight will be of God. I don't want you to tell me anything. What I have shared up this point was not specifically for your church, it was for the pastors that were visiting (about 20 pastors). Tonight all those pastors will have left and they won't be there. The message tonight is for you and your church."

When we got to church that night, Pastor Green was right. There was not one visiting pastor there. His title for the message that night was, *"Yes, We Can. Yes, We Will."* The theme of the message was challenging us to arise and build. At the end of the service, he spoke the following prophetic word over my life.

November 15, 1985 – Prophetic Word Given Through Rev. Charles Green to Russell McCollough

> *This is the way, walk ye in it.....*
>
> *Oh Son, I have called you unto this place for this time. I have called you here because I have fashioned and prepared a people for my namesake and my glory.*
>
> *I am going to put my understanding within you, such as it has never been before; and I am going to make you an astute man to recognize the moving of God, and to be able to smell trouble before it even gets here and to fashion a defense against it.*

Do not be afraid of the faces of the people, for God Almighty shall deliver you from the people to whom He will send you, even as He did the Apostle Paul.

For behold, the people are in need of a man who will rise up and say: "This is the way, walk ye in it." Therefore do not be afraid to hear my Word and then, stand before my people without apology and say: "The Living God has spoken to me and thus has He spoken and thus shall we do."

For the anointing of the Lord God within you, shall destroy yokes and bondages, and because of you, many captive sons and daughters shall be set free. For my Word is not only in you, but my power is within your hand. And even as my hand does burn with the anointing of God, even so, in the midst of the anointing, this hand that I hold shall begin to burn in your palm and it shall be a sign unto you, not unto others, but unto you.

And you shall know that it is healing time. It is delivering time. And you shall lay your hands upon the sick and upon the destitute, and upon the fearful; and they shall be transformed by the laying on of your hands and by the Word that shall come forth out of my mouth, says the Living God. Therefore, fear not to put my Word into operation.

Pastor Green also had a prophetic word to the church as follows:

Thus says the Lord to this church: There is an authority in your relationship with Jesus Christ. It is time for you to rise up and live out the mandate that has been given to you by Almighty God and say: "YES, I CAN."

For the Lord your God shall become creative in your midst to bless you. He shall bless you in ways that you have never dreamed possible. He shall move the obstructions out of your way and He shall cause people that have the ability to help you to rally to your side and to your cause and He will begin to work on your behalf.

For the Lord will cause His miracle power to rest upon this church. He will cause His glory to be in this place and there will begin to come forth a touch of God upon you and upon this place so that people shall walk through this door with infirmities and in the midst of the glory and in the midst of the praise and worship, they shall be transformed. They shall be healed, and they shall go forth and publish that which has happened to them. And the word shall begin to be spread abroad, and it shall begin to be said that: "God is in that house."

The Lord would have you to begin to prepare yourself by understanding His Word and seeking His face and recognizing that it is He that has brought you this far. It is not your conniving, it is not your cleverness, it is not your public relations' ability; but it is the Lord your God that has brought you to this place. And the God who has brought you this far is able to do marvelous things that you have dared only to dream about. Therefore, let your heart be transformed and let your mind be changed. Begin to think as God would have you to think. And say: "The Lord will greatly multiply us!"

I see a vision as I am talking to you right now. I see people rushing out of this place and rushing into every area in this whole general vicinity and you are rushing with excitement out of this place to share what God is doing here. And you are saying to people: "Surely, now after you have heard my report, you will want to come with me to the House of God."

And you shall find that as you shall believe the Word and put it into operation that there shall be an increase that shall be amazing to you. And God will use this increase and begin to force you to hear the command to be blessed and to say: "All that the Lord has said we will do" Do not be afraid of the moving of God. For there are others who have rejected my move and they have died in their tracks. But I have not plans of death for you, but I have plans of life. Therefore, rise up, hear the Word of the Lord and be profited by His Word, says the Living God.

Needless to say, following that church service, I was overwhelmed with the graciousness of God and felt that I could climb any mountain and scale any height. Our church family had been given a huge spiritual boost.

Later I took Pastor Green out for refreshment and he shared with me that God had impressed upon him to come back and help us with a fundraising campaign to buy some property. He also said he would send a couple to us – a businessman and his wife from New Orleans who would come and help us. With their help, within four months we had begun a fundraising campaign to raise the funds to pay cash for property on which to build a new church.

We immediately began looking for property hoping to find at least five acres upon which to build a new sanctuary. It was 1986 and land was very valuable in Roseville. The lowest price we could find was $600,000 per acre.

It became my custom to look for property whenever I had the opportunity. One day I was driving around when I saw a 4' x

8' sign advertising 20 acres for sale at the edge of the city limits. I wrote down the phone number when I returned to my office and called the listing realtor whose name was Steve. I asked him how much the property was and he said $200,000. I thought he meant $200,000 per acre however, he meant the whole 20 acres for $200,000.

I became very excited until he informed me that he had just received an offer for the property. I asked him if I could put a backup offer on the property but he told me that it was a very firm proposal that involved five businessmen. Steve contacted me the following week and told me that their offer was definitely accepted. I asked him to find out if they were interested in selling and if so to present them a price of $400,000 for the 20 acres. They rejected our offer so I informed him to offer them more. They rejected my second offer and Steve informed me they were not interested in selling as they were going to develop the property into a housing community.

A couple of days later I drove to where the 20 acres was located and parked my pickup on the side of the road. I walked about 50 yards into the open field that was knee-high with grass and knelt down and began to pray. I questioned God as to why we had missed this piece of property and asked Him for a creative idea and an offer amount that I could propose that would be acceptable to the owners. I told the Lord I was returning to my office and by the time I arrived there I wanted that creative idea because I was going to call Steve and make another offer.

I then reached down and took some of the dirt into my hands, stood up on my feet and threw it in the air and shouted, "*I declare this is holy ground.*" I turned to walk back to my pickup and as I looked down I saw a snake. I have one reaction when it comes to snakes – I run. I will even run from a rubber snake when I know it's a rubber snake. As I stood there, I began to look around for a weapon and noticed a 2x4 board about five feet long. I picked up the board and began to hit the snake. I hit the snake until it stopped moving and then I hit it some more. I tossed the board away and then I walked straight towards the snake and stepped over it.

As I proceeded to my car, I heard the Lord speak to me and say, "*You will do battle with the serpent but you will win.*"

When I got to my pickup, I had no idea what I was going to tell Steve. When I got to my office I still didn't have any idea. When I greeted my secretary, I had no idea what I was going to say. I picked up the phone and dialed the number and asked for Steve. I still had no idea what I was going to say. When he said, "Hello," immediately I knew what to say.

I said, "Steve, I want to make another offer on the property."

He said, "Rev. McCollough they are not interested in selling – I would be embarrassed to take another offer to them."

I said," If you don't take this offer to them I will use another realtor."

He replied, "Okay, what have you got?"

I said, "Write up an offer for ten acres – total price $150,000 to be paid in cash one year from date of acceptance."

He never said a word for about 20 seconds.

I said, "Steve, are you there?"

He said, "Okay, I'll do it."

Steve called me a week later to inform me that we had just bought ten acres and that the owners agreed to wait for one year to receive our cash payment. I asked Steve why they didn't take the previous offers but they took my last offer which was lower. He said, "When you told me to make that offer I knew that you did not know what they owed on the 20 acres. They accepted your offer because they still owed $150,000. By accepting your offer it gave them ten acres free and clear and they do not want their money until a year from now because of a potential tax issue."

Wow! God really does know how to build a church if we let him.

We were still in our fundraising campaign but, after one year we had accumulated $200,000 in the building fund and were ready to pay off the land.

The following day after we received title to the property, I called Steve and asked him if he had ever sold a church. He said he never had but he would do some comparables with other commercial buildings with limited use and get back to me. We thought if we could get $200,000 for our current 80 year old church in a land-locked location, we would be very excited.

That same afternoon I heard a knock on the church door and when I went to answer it, I found three people in uniform standing there. The man in charge of the group said, "We would like to know if you are interested in selling your church."

I said, "Yes, did Steve send you here?"

He replied, "No, we do not know a Steve."

I invited them in and they looked the church building over without saying a word, then they thanked me and left. Two weeks later, I accepted an offer from the Salvation Army Organization in the amount of $550,000 cash for our church. We now had ten acres paid for and $600,000 in our building fund.

After we sold our church, we needed a building in which to hold church services. We made arrangements with The Salvation Army to rent our former building and hold our main service on Sunday afternoon whereas they would hold their service on Sunday morning. They were great folks to rent from and we gained a real appreciation for The Salvation Army Organization.

After one year of renting from The Salvation Army, we decided to rent another church building in Roseville – then known as Key to Life Christian Fellowship but now known as Living Way. Our friends, Randy and Karen Luke, were the lead pastors and they graciously gave us every consideration while we used their facilities for approximately one year. We were indeed blessed by our association with the Salvation Army and Key to Life during the two years we spent building our new church.

Chapter 14 – New Church Completed

Building the new church, the lengthy delays in getting it completed and the stress involved took a toll on our congregation, especially me. As most people are aware, when you decide to build, you must first count the cost – to my way of thinking, it is a good idea to double the cost. Since this was our first building project, we believed that we had truly counted the cost but we certainly didn't double it and we ran out of funds before our building was complete.

A couple of subs overcharged us and a few subs were somewhat dishonest but mostly, things just cost a lot more than what we had counted on. The delays we encountered contributed to more expense and frustration.

Thankfully, we were blessed with a great general contractor and he worked with us until we ran out of funds. Then, we released him while we considered how we could complete our facility.

During that time, Satan harassed me with the thought – *"Yes, you took the people into the Wilderness but you can't get them into the Promised Land."* I constantly fought doubts and struggled with *"What if's?"*

Charlie Cagle, a faithful friend of mine and one of our church leaders, would leave his place of business each afternoon and meet me at the church. Together we were able to complete a few projects. More important than the work we performed, his friendship and companionship was a great source of encouragement to me.

Finally, after the building just sat there with little progress being made for nearly a year, we began another stewardship program and hired an individual in our church to supervise volunteer teams to do whatever we could do. We hired out the rest of the work as we obtained the funds to complete the project.

Many of our church members laid carpet, tile, glued baseboard, put up sheet rock, painted walls, stained cabinets and cleaned up after those who were working. This job was greatly complicated because so many people had no experience doing such work – they were simply willing workers who wanted their church to be completed. I jokingly promised our church family I would perform a backward flip off the platform during our first service in the new building.

In August, 1992 we were able to get our final permit to occupy our church building at 8330 Brady Lane in Roseville, California. The main sanctuary was built to seat 500 people with overflow areas seating an additional 200. We had sizeable classrooms for all ages of children, a fellowship hall that seated 200 and an administration wing. The building was a total of 22,000 square feet.

We held our first service in the building on August 9th and needless to say, our congregation was in a celebratory mood. Just before I began to preach my sermon, the drummer began doing a drum roll. People began saying, "Do it – do it."

I responded, "Do what?" Then they reminded me about the backward flip I had promised to do. Before I could back out, I gathered up my courage, told everyone to stand back and proceeded to do a backward flip off the platform as I had promised many months previously. Some people said they didn't see it so I had to do a second one. Judy and some of the more sensible people in the congregation were just thankful I didn't break my neck – *SO WAS I!*

In November of that year we held dedication services for our new building and asked our dear friend, Pastor Charles Green to come and officiate. We celebrated with our church family and guests with gladness of heart.

Chapter 15 – The Exodus

We were very relieved to occupy our new building at long last. However, our journey had not been an easy one and it would take a drastic toll on our congregation in the months to come.

Even though we were mentally and physically weary, we were experiencing a great move of God in our services. People were lining up to receive ministry and there were some remarkable testimonies of God's work in individual lives.

Then, the unthinkable happened. In all our years of pastoring we had never experienced a mass exodus. However, three short months after we moved into our new building, people began leaving. Over a three month period, we had 80 – 100 members leave the church. A variety of reasons were given as people departed – some wanted to attend a church that was taking a different direction than our church was taking. As I mentioned earlier, we had previously made some changes in our services and not everyone was in agreement with those changes. Others didn't give a reason – they just left.

As I have looked back upon this period of my life, I realize the majority of the people who left didn't have hard feelings toward the leadership of our church; perhaps they simply wanted a fresh start for their families.

Although I didn't want to dwell on it at the time, Judy and I were not perfect pastors and had most certainly made our share of mistakes during our tenure as lead pastors. In such cases, the congregation bears the brunt of the failures and mistakes of leadership. Among those who left, were also those who were disillusioned by our leadership. Whatever the reasons people departed, it was a very tough pill to swallow.

Several of the folks that left were in key leadership positions as well as faithful financial givers. The exodus came at a bad time – we were already struggling to meet our mortgage payments. But more painful than the concern about our church finances was the wounding and rejection I was suffering in my soul.

I would absolutely dread receiving a phone call and hearing these words on the other end of the line: "Pastor Russell could my wife and I arrange to meet with you?" I began to have a literal pain in my chest and thought I might be having heart problems.

So many folks left that some of our leaders were performing double duty during our services and since they all had secular jobs as well as serving in the church, it was indeed a laborious season in our lives.

Our family was heartsick as we watched family after family depart – many were couples for whom I had performed marriages, baptisms and baby dedications. We could barely hold our heads up and wondered who would be the next to leave. Through it all, we knew we could not hold an offense against those who were leaving. Many of them had been friends for many years. We wanted to preserve our relationships with them as much as possible.

One Sunday morning, Judy told Christa and Angela, "No matter how we feel, we will put on our brightest clothes, go to church and hold our heads up." And, indeed, we did.

Our family was not alone in our struggle. Our key leaders who stayed with us were having struggles of their own, especially since some had family members who were part of the exodus. Through it all, they remained faithful and steadfast and stuck with us through thick and thin. Only pastors who have gone through such a time could understand the value of these good people.

Judy and I have often said that we would never have been able to pastor without the following families – The Quezadas, The Cagles, The Taylors, The Shenefields, The Glasgows, The Austins, The Beanes, The Hamletts and many others including our own two lovely daughters, Christa and Angela. Although it was easy to look at the negative, we also had the positive element of those who remained with us and continued steadfast as we ministered to one another and the congregation each week.

For a six month period after the departure, Christa led worship every Sunday morning and in addition taught Children's Church. Of course, she had help but there was a strong responsibility in these ministries that fell upon her shoulders. She was 22 years old at the time but she was a seasoned laborer – wise beyond her years.

One outstanding young couple, Bill and Missy Taylor, had secular jobs and young children but there was never a more faithful family than these two. Bill had been our lead worship leader for several years but we were now without a drummer so he drummed each Sunday while Christa led worship. Like all of us, Bill did whatever needed to be done for the benefit of all.

Finally, after several months, Judy and I were blessed to be able to take a few days' vacation. We flew to the New

England states and drove mile after mile as we attempted to accept God's healing grace into our wounded souls.

The trip did seem to help but the pain in my chest continued to persist for several months. Later, an EKG revealed a "possible" heart attack but it was never confirmed – doctors expressed a difference of opinion regarding this test.

Things seemed to level out in time. There was more than one Sunday that we brought the financial needs before the congregation – seemingly vast amounts for the size of our church. Often we needed to receive as much as $10,000 on a given Sunday in order to meet our budget. At this time, we had less than 200 people in our congregation.

Although we didn't speak the words out loud, we were concerned that we might lose our church building. Indeed, we realized the church is more than a building made of hands – but we felt a huge weight of responsibility to those who had given so generously and labored so diligently during this journey.

One Sunday when we three months behind in our mortgage payments – approximately $40,000 – we received a miraculous offering in the amount of $44,000 which enabled us to catch up on all our outstanding bills.

God was moving in a powerful way across the land and in our services. We continued in our efforts to have seasoned outside ministers come in for special services and our congregation was greatly blessed by the words spoken over their lives individually and corporately.

One major happening during this season was the Sunday a young man came to our church on a mission to meet Christa.

He had heard about her from mutual friends and decided to come and see what was so special about this girl.

It didn't take long for him to find out what made Christa so "special" and within a few short months, we welcomed Don Proctor as our first son-in-law. He was a responsible, stable, kindhearted young man from a fine family. Confident in his own person, he would ultimately prove to be one of Christa's biggest encouragers in her ministry as she continued to teach, preach, sing – whatever God called her to do. We found him to be one in a million.

As a young adult, Angela made the decision to go into The State Park Peace Officer Cadet Ranger/Lifeguard Training. She moved to Monterey for her training and after her successful graduation, she went to work at Lake Perris in Southern California.

While there she met and married Marc Milligan – a capable, kindhearted man. Marc brought along a special blessing into our family – a sweet little daughter – Ashley Autumn, age five years old, from his previous marriage. In 2001, Marc, Angela and Ashley moved from Southern California to the Roseville area.

Yes, there were some changes taking place in our lives and although many of the changes were wonderful, I was having a great internal struggle. I was wounded and the wounds I was suffering were not just related to the present, I was still suffering from the effects of my childhood as well.

Chapter 16 – The Bruise

There seems to be a paradox. A person can be touched by Almighty God's power as in my case with the miracle of my youth, yet be left with a bruise which will continue to cause pain. My bruise was a fear – a fear of once again being abandoned or rejected by friends and/or family. Most of my adult life I had become supersensitive and easily wounded but I thought I was good at covering this bruise. I tried very hard to please people. I wanted everyone to like me. I simply could not understand if they didn't. I'm sure that most of the time they did like and accept me, but my vain imagination was causing a pain in my bruise.

It always seemed to me that my bruise was more easily exposed among those that were the nearest and dearest to my heart. Judy and I could have a disagreement over anything and I would sense the pain of my bruise telling me, *"This is the beginning of the end. She is rejecting me. She doesn't love me."* And there were times I felt she was confronting me to build up a reason to leave me. All of this of course was a lie.

During the 20 years I served in the role of Senior Pastor I tried to cover up the pain of the bruise. This happened more times than I care to remember. For example, while I would be ministering, a person would leave their pew and go out the back door perhaps to go to the restroom and I would interpret that as a rejection. I would start thinking – *"They're leaving because they don't like what I said and they probably won't be back."* Added to those types of situations, there were some church members who were very disrespectful and insensitive during the first couple of years I pastored.

For example, on some occasions immediately following the Sunday morning church service, a couple of members would walk up and shake hands with me and hand me a piece of paper. This paper would contain a grade for my sermon that Sunday. Most of the grades were a C+ or C. Sometimes I would receive a D but I never got an A. These were good friends and even though they meant it as a joke – a very cynical joke – but a joke nonetheless, I knew they were trying to get a point across as well.

My friends did not know they were putting their finger on a very sore bruise as I felt the pain of rejection. I needed to be set free from this bruise but at the time I wasn't fully aware of how to go about the process of receiving my healing.

I now realize that most of my life was filled with unreal expectations. When my expectations were not fulfilled, I became very disappointed. Disappointment leads to discouragement. Discouragement leads to depression and then I was in a position for the enemy of my soul to steal the truth and insert a lie. The lie became my reality. I thought I was covering my bruise very well. Looking back upon those years, I now realize that there were others, especially those close to me, who were aware of my struggles. But, it was difficult for me to receive anything positive. I was afraid to let go and trust because I feared any disappointment. You see, when you have an unrelenting bruise in your soul, you are in a painful prison.

I came to a place where I heard something snap inside of me. I thought, *"I can't take it anymore."* I basically gave up and opened myself up to some stupid decisions in my personal life and ministry. I take full responsibility for all that began to happen to me, to my family and the church.

In December 1998, after 20 years of serving as Senior Pastor, I resigned from the church and came very close to losing my family. My marriage began to fall apart and there were times I found myself isolated and having a pity party. It seemed now that the rejection from people just multiplied. I waited for phone calls from certain people to encourage me that never came. The enemy of my soul was taking advantage of this dire situation and I allowed him to bruise me up even more but the bottom line was, I found myself in a prison (the bruise) and I needed to be set free.

Luke NKJV - 4:16 – 21 says:

16 So He came to Nazareth, where He had been brought up. And as His custom was, He went into the synagogue on the Sabbath day, and stood up to read.
17 And He was handed the book of the prophet Isaiah. And when He had opened the book, He found the place where it was written:

18 The Spirit of the Lord is upon Me,
Because He has anointed Me
To preach the gospel to the poor;
He has sent Me to heal the brokenhearted,
To proclaim liberty to the captives
And recovery of sight to the blind,
To set at liberty those who are oppressed.
19 To proclaim the acceptable year of the Lord.
20 Then He closed the book, and gave it back to the attendant and sat down. And the eyes of all who were in the synagogue were fixed on Him.

When Jesus read from the book of Isaiah he listed six things that he was anointed to do. The fifth thing He was anointed to do was to set at liberty those who were oppressed. The translators of the King James Version stated it this way, *"To set at liberty those who are bruised."* For application purposes I will use the King James Version. If the translators had written, *"to set at liberty those who are in prison or in jail,* or to have translated, *to heal those who are bruised,"* that connotation would have made more sense. To *set at liberty those who are bruised* – this indicates that if you have a bruise, you are in captivity and need to be set free.

A natural bruise is a bleed on the inside of your body. You can cover it up with clothing or make-up and no one will be able to see it but, you will know it's there. It is a very embarrassing mark and sometimes very painful and especially if someone touches it. There are many people today – even Christians who are walking around with emotional, spiritual, and social bruises.

These bruises exist in their soul because of hurtful circumstances in their past. There are many ways people receive emotional or spiritual bruises. Perhaps they were verbally, emotionally or physically abused in their past. Maybe they were offended or they offended someone and find themselves unable to get over the circumstance surrounding the offense. Perhaps they got into an unhealthy environment and their expectations were not fulfilled and now they're wounded and bruised. Then again, maybe like me, they were wounded in their early childhood because of abandonment, neglect and rejection by biological parents as well as rejection by peers during most of my childhood.

During this most difficult time in my life, I found I still had a lot of fight in me and I determined that I would fight my way back from the pit I was now in. Even though it was often hard and somewhat depressing to face my day, I resolved I would make every effort to make each day count for something.

Chapter 17 – Set Free

Judy and I decided on a separation while we made an attempt to work out the issues that had led us to this dark place in our lives. We began to seek counsel and God blessed us to be able to regularly meet with Don Phillips, a professional counselor from San Jose and Pastor Francis and Suzie Anfuso from the Rock of Roseville. God used these wonderful people to help us rebuild our marriage and after a few weeks, we reunited.

I will never forget something that Francis said to me. He said, "Russell you must know that Jesus plus zero is enough. You must know that it is only important what Jesus thinks about you." Most of my life I had known that fact to be true. However I only had head knowledge and not heart knowledge. Maybe it was because I was so desperate for any hope but I grabbed onto that statement and would not let it go. When the reality of that statement took residence inside my heart, it was as if I could see Jesus standing at the door of my prison with the keys in his hand.

When Judy and I resigned as pastors, our son-in-law Don, and our daughter, Christa, being confirmed by the church eldership and congregation, stepped into the role of Lead Pastors of the church.

Not wanting to detract from their leadership, we felt it best to attend elsewhere, allowing time for them to become established in their leadership roles while we focused on the restoration of our marriage.

For the next 18 months we attended the Rock of Roseville

with Pastor Francis Anfuso and Suzie and their congregation. In 2000 after our first grandchild, Danielle, was born; Judy and I received the blessing of Pastor Francis to return to the church where we had pastored for so many years. The congregation welcomed us back with open arms.

During this period, Christa was working outside the home as well as helping Don to pastor the church. It was my privilege to become one of Danielle's primary caregivers while her parents were working. I look back upon those days and realize they were some of the most precious times in my life. A very strong bond developed between Danielle and me. I knew one thing – I loved her and she loved me – we had a total acceptance of each other. Little did I know that God was going to use Danielle to teach me something about His love and acceptance.

I had already made a quality choice that if this child or any of my immediate family was in any danger, I would stand in the line of fire and die for them if necessary. I would not have to waste a millimeter of a second to decide what to do – my mind was firmly made up.

One particular day I will never forget. Danielle was about 12 months old. Like any other day, I would spend a lot of time teaching her how to walk and talk. Danielle never had a dull moment when she was in my care – we were always engaged in activities or playing together. That afternoon as I was bouncing her in my lap, I heard the Lord speak to me and say, "Do you think she loves you?"

I said, “Oh God, I know she loves me.”

He asked again, “Do you think she really loves you?”

I replied, “Yes God, I know she really loves me.”

He then asked me a question I'll never forget. He asked, “Do you love her?”

I answered, “Oh yes God, I really love her.”

He then said, “How much do you love her?"

I said, “I would give my life for her.”

He said, “So you know how much you love her?”

I said “Yes.”

Then He said, “I love you and I have already given my life for you.”

That encounter completely opened up my understanding of how much God loved me. I remember weeping until the laughter came.

A few days later as Judy and I were in bed asleep, I heard my name called, “Russell.” I immediately awakened, sat up in bed and looked around but no one else was in the room and Judy was asleep. The room was quiet so I lay back down and in the twilight of my sleep I heard my name called again. I sat up, looked around and after sitting there for awhile, I lay back down to go to sleep again.

As I was about to go to sleep, I heard my name called out again the third time, only much louder. This time I got out of bed and walked through the house to see if someone was there. I came back to the bedroom and put a blanket around my shoulders and walked outside and sat on one of the patio chairs.

As I sat there, I said, "God is that you? What do you want?"

He said, "I just woke you up to spend a little time with you."

I thought to myself, "Wow, the Maker of the universe woke me up to spend a little time with me."

We then had a very loving conversation and when it was over I knew that this anointed one had come to set me free. There are those who will say that God does not speak to people. But, the Bible says, *"My sheep hear my voice and a stranger they will not follow."* I know this for certain as the old song says: *"He walks with me and He talks with me and He tells me I am his own and the joys we share as we tarry there none other has ever known."* The anointed one was there and he set me free from my bruise. Now, I am free. I am free and I don't care what you think of me. Who the son of man has set free, is free indeed. This one thing I have found to be true – Jesus plus zero is enough.

Shortly after this experience, I received a phone call from a very good friend, Pastor John Weigelt, from Carson, California. He informed me that I had been on his mind. He was unaware of the current circumstances in my life. Throughout my life I had covered the bruise very well. As we talked, I informed him that I had resigned from pastoring our church. John was very supportive in every way. He then contacted another pastor friend, Murray Galloway, who pastors a church in Pontotoc, Mississippi. Murray began to call me and encourage me also.

There are no words to express the amount of support and encouragement these men of God have given to me. While I was pastoring, they had called upon me several times to come and minister in their respective churches. Although I was no longer pastoring, both John and Murray asked me to come and minister to their congregations. It has been my pleasure to go and speak in their pulpits at special meetings, conferences and weekend services during the past 12 years. This was one of the way in which it was confirmed to me that God wasn't finished with me and the call of God.

During the same season that John and Murray called, I received a phone call from our very dear pastor friend, Charles Green, who had been very instrumental in the lives of our family and church.

Pastor Green is well known for the prophetic anointing in his ministry. As far as I know, he knew nothing about what Judy and I had been experiencing. He said to me, "Russell, God spoke to me and told me to call you and tell you your feet are still beautiful. I don't know what that means to you personally right now, but I'm sure you do."

Immediately Isaiah 52:7 came to my mind. It reads, *"How beautiful upon the mountains are the feet of him who brings good news."* That Word from the Lord confirmed to me that God was not finished using me in the ministry. Pastor Green has continued to be a great help and encouragement to me.

Chapter 18 – Four Corners Ministries

After I resigned from pastoring and once Judy and I were on our path to recovery in our marriage, I had the assurance that God was not finished with me and perhaps it was time to allow that long held desire to come to fruition – traveling and ministering in the U.S. and other areas of the world.

As I pondered this new course of action, I would often think of an experience I had a few years previously. In 1995 Judy and I were attending a conference in Yuba City, California where Prophet Kim Clement was ministering. After his sermon, Kim began to speak very accurate prophetic words to some of those in attendance. He picked me out of the congregation and asked me to come forward. As he spoke, he confirmed that I had long desired to travel to other nations; that God had given me an excellent family and that I would travel to the four corners of the earth.

Finally, it seemed the right time to take action on this long held dream. In March of 2000, we set up a nonprofit 501 (c) 3 corporation – a missions organization and named it Four Corners Ministries. The name came in part from the prophetic word I had received from Kim Clement and also the scripture found in Isaiah 11:12: *"He will set up a banner for the nations............from the FOUR CORNERS of the earth."*

In my travels I have been to several countries including Canada, China, Switzerland, Italy, Romania, Mexico, Trinidad, British Guyana, Ecuador, and to most of the states in the union. Most of the ministry on behalf of Four Corners consists of teaching seminars, workshops and general ministry to local churches. Whenever possible we have taken teaching manuals such as Bibles, concordances, computer equipment and gifts of money to ministries in third world countries.

For a few years, one of the major focuses of Four Corners' ministry was to the nation of Trinidad where I ministered alongside Bishop Anthony Kawalsingh. These have been some of the most enjoyable times of my traveling ministry.

I have a statement that speaks the intent of my heart. *It was said of Jesus that He was anointed by God with the Holy Spirit and Power and that He went about doing good and healing all that were OPPRESSED* (Acts 10:38). It is my desire to minister to people and to make a positive difference in their lives and to see them liberated from all their bruises. By the grace of God, we endeavor to help people to:

- Rise to a higher level of faith
- Realize a greater commitment to Christ
- Have a positive attitude
- Enjoy a deeper intimacy with Christ
- Win the fight and help people to make a difference in their own sphere of influence.

Chapter 19 – Maintaining Your Liberty

In this section, I would like to share some of the principles I have found to be helpful in my own life as I have sought to maintain the liberty that has come to be so precious to me. Whenever I am asked to speak in a church where I have not previously ministered, I share my personal testimony of the wounds and bruises I have struggled with and how I have been liberated from the "bruise." I then give this follow-up sermon titled "Maintaining Your Liberty."

Galatians 5:1 – *"Stand fast therefore in the liberty by which Christ has made us free, and do not be entangled again with a yoke of bondage."*

To become liberated is one thing but, to remain liberated is yet another. Just like our judicial system, many prisoners have been set free only to find themselves back in prison again. They failed to keep the proper attitude and lifestyle in order to maintain their liberty. So, we who have allowed the anointed one to liberate us from the bruise must also contend to maintain our liberty. I do not have all the answers neither can I exhaust this subject, but I have some suggestions that have helped me.

1) Get Rid of the Darkness

Satan loves darkness. When Satan was cast out of heaven due to his rebellion, he went to planet earth perhaps because it was dark. This possibly happened between Genesis Chapter 1, Verse 1 and Verse 2. In Genesis 2, the Bible says that *"darkness covered the face of the deep."*

We do know that Satan was present upon the earth, because it was then that he tempted Adam and Eve and they committed the sin of disobedience which brought the curse upon mankind. If anyone has darkness in their life, Satan has a Biblical and legal right to dwell there.

Satan and his minions are referred to as the rulers of darkness. In Ephesians 6:12 the Bible says – *"For we do not wrestle against flesh and blood, but against principalities, against powers, against the rulers of darkness of this age, against spiritual hosts of wickedness in the heavenly places."*

The works of darkness can be described as the works of the flesh shown in Galatians 5: 19 -21, *"Now the works of the flesh are evident, which are adultery, fornication, uncleanness, lewdness, idolatry, sorcery, hatred, contentions, jealousies, outbursts of wrath, selfish ambitions, dissentions, heresies, envy, murders, drunkenness, revelries, and the like of which I tell you beforehand, just as I also told you in time past, that those who practice such things will not inherit the kingdom of God."*

God hates darkness but He loves the light. The first thing that God did when He began to form the earth was to get rid of the darkness. When He said, *"Let there be light,"* immediately, the darkness was pierced by the Words that He spoke.

The Bible says that the Word of God will not return to him void for He watches over it to perform what He sent it to do (Isaiah 55:11). When God said, *"Let there be light,"* light began to pierce the darkness at the speed of 186,000 miles per second. That is equivalent to 669,600,000 miles per hour. That should give us an idea of how much God hates darkness and loves the light. Since God spoke that word, *"Let there be light,"* light is still piercing the darkness today. Remember He is watching over his Word to perform it.

You get rid of the darkness by letting in the light. The light will always break through the darkness.

The way you let the light in is by:

- Reading His Word
- Engaging in fervent prayer
- Keeping your thoughts pure
- Involving yourself in praise and worship
- Keeping your conversation clean
- Witnessing about the goodness of God to others
- Repent of all your sins and wrongdoing, and
- Live and walk in the fruit of the spirit as defined in Galatians 5:22-23 – *"But the fruit of the Spirit is love, joy, peace, longsuffering, kindness, goodness, faithfulness, gentleness, self-control. Against such there is no law."*

In Isaiah 61:3 we read that praise and worship will remove the spirit of heaviness. Tommy Tenney gave a great example of the benefits of involving oneself in praise and worship in his book, "The God Chasers.[2]"

He used an example of how older houses would have a single light built in the center of the room with a string hanging down. When you pulled on the string you would turn the light on. However, once in awhile you might come into a dark room and be unable to find the light string. You might then walk around the room looking up, waving your arms around trying to find the means to turn the light on.

When an uninformed person comes into church during the praise and worship portion of the service and sees people waving their arms around and perhaps some of them acting in a boisterous manner, the uninformed person might ask, *"What are they doing?"* The answer might be, *"They are trying to turn the light on."* I do believe that praise and worship produces Godly joy and that joy is our strength (Nehemiah 8:10). We must have that strength to win the battle.

#2) You Must Choose Your Battles

One day I overheard my son-in-law, Don Proctor, make a statement to someone. He said, "You just have to choose your battles." That is another way of saying, *"Don't sweat the small stuff."* Many times, there have been people who chose to win the battle only to lose the war. The price of winning the battle may be too great.

I have been active in the ministry for over 40 years. Many times I have had people come to me and say, "Pastor, I have a problem." Before it was over the person had described his problem as his wife. His wife then described her problem as her husband. The children would say the parents were the problem. The parents together would describe their children as the problem. Others would describe their problem as their employer or their employees or their neighbor.

One day as I was praying for all of these people, I asked the Lord what a problem was. I was inspired to look up the word "problem" in Webster's dictionary. One of the ways he defined a problem was: *"something that bothers you."* I took that to mean that if it did not bother you, you might not have a problem. What may bother one person may not bother another, therefore – what may be a problem to one may not be a problem to another.

One day I was driving down the road on my way to either perform a wedding or officiate at a funeral. All I can recall is – I had my burying and marrying suit on. I hadn't eaten yet so I decided it would be a good idea to grab a bite. I pulled into Carl's Jr. and ordered a juicy hamburger, fries and a Diet Coke. As I am driving down the road, enjoying my hamburger, I notice that a messy pickle had dropped out of my hamburger and landed on my pants. I call this the "pickle on the pants" story.

I had become so engrossed in cleaning the pickle off my pants and continuing to eat the hamburger and fries and drink my Diet Coke that I was not paying much attention to my driving. Suddenly I heard a loud air horn. I looked up and my vehicle had drifted to the wrong side of the road and I was about to have a head on collision with a great big 18 wheeler truck. Suddenly, the pickle on the pants was no longer a problem. The pickle on the pants was not bothering me anymore. I made a decision to choose my battle. I think I chose the right one.

Also, regarding your problems, I like the following statement, "Your problem is not your problem, it's what you do about it that is your problem." When it comes to making a quality decision and we don't allow ourselves to be bothered or irritated, it is then made easier to choose the right battle. I don't know if it's possible, but it would be great if we never had any battles because we didn't allow anything to bother us. In order to maintain my liberty, I have asked God for His grace in my life so that I may abide by the following guideline: *"It is not what you say in life, it is how you say it. It is not all in what you do, it is how you do it. But, more importantly how do you make people feel?*

II Corinthians 10:3-6 – *"For though we walk in the flesh, we do not war according to the flesh. For the weapons of our warfare are not carnal but mighty in God for the pulling down of strongholds, casting down arguments and every high thing that exalts itself against the knowledge of God, bringing every thought into captivity to the obedience of Christ. And being made ready to punish all disobedience when your obedience is fulfilled."*

#3) Never Give Up

You are not a failure unless you choose to give up. Many people have heard me say, ***"I'm not down, I'm either up or getting up."*** No one is perfect. The only people in the Bible that were recorded as being perfect were translated. If you are alive and on planet earth, guess what – you are probably not perfect. **We are to make up our mind and put it in our heart that we will never give up**.

On October 29, 1941, the Prime Minister of Great Britain, Winston Churchill, made a speech at Harrow School where he attended as a youth. The following is part of the speech he made. *"The pessimist sees the problem in every opportunity. Whereas the optimist sees the opportunity in every problem. Never give in. Never give in. Never! Never! Never!! Never!!! In nothing great or small, large or petty, never give in except to conviction of honor and good sense. Never yield to force. Never yield to the apparent overwhelming might of the enemy."*

That was the attitude he had that helped England and the Allies defeat Nazi Germany in World War II.

In your fight to maintain your liberty, when the devil comes to remind you of your past, just remind him of his future. There is a great confession that Israel made and you can make it also. Micah 7:8 – *"Do not rejoice over me my enemy. When I fall, I will arise. When I sit in darkness the Lord will be a light to me."*

Never give up! I love the Apostle Paul's valedictory in II Timothy 4:7-8 – *"I have fought a good fight, I have finished the race, I have kept the faith. Finally there is laid up for me the crown of righteousness which the Lord the righteous judge will give to me on that day and not to me only but also to all who have loved his appearing."*

I call this my three amigos – **Fight, Finish and Keep**. Those three friends will help you maintain your liberty.

The Word of God tells us that God will not tempt us, but He will test us. Sometimes the test is long and hard and we cry out, "God where are you? I can't hear you?" Just like in school, perhaps the teacher is quiet during the test. But always remember, it is an open book test. We have the written Word of God called the Bible. Eventually we hear the teacher (Master) say, "Okay, time is up."

You may not be successful in one area but don't give up. When you experience failure in an area, you may find that you are very successful in another area. I remember hearing a story about a young boy who picked up his baseball and bat and went to his back yard declaring that he was the greatest hitter of all time. He tossed the ball up in front of him and swung the bat and missed, "Strike One!" He picked up the ball and pitched it up in front of him and swung the second time and missed, "Strike Two!" He muttered to himself, "I am the greatest baseball hitter of all time!" Once again he picked up the ball and tossed it up and swung his bat and missed, "Strike Three!" He then threw down the bat and picked up the ball, looked at it in amazement and said, "Wow, I am the greatest pitcher of all time!"

To maintain my liberty, I used my competitive nature and refused to give up. Winston Churchill was right. We can be an optimist and see the opportunity in every problem.

#4) Close the Gate

There is a cardinal rule that says whenever you walk through a closed door or gate; you should close that gate after you pass through. As we go through life, there are many experiences that we must leave in the past. We cannot reside in the graveyard of past failures nor can we live in the smoke of yesterday's fire. The Apostle Paul wrote in Philippians 3:12-14 – *"Brethren, I do not count myself to have apprehended but one thing I do,* ***forgetting those things which are behind*** *and reaching forward to those things which are ahead. I press toward the goal for the prize of the upward call of God in Christ Jesus."*

To close the gate means to leave your past behind – the mistakes and the disappointments in your past that will continue to haunt you and cause you to lose yourself, your confidence and the hope of a great future. For these reasons, you must close that gate.

In the book of Genesis, Chapters 37 through chapter 50, we read the story of Joseph. Joseph is misunderstood by his brothers. They hated him and abused him and put him in a pit. They sold him to the Midianites who then sold him to Potiphar in the land of Egypt. Potiphar's wife tried to seduce him but he fled from her only to be lied about and cast into prison. While in prison for approximately 9 years, he met the butler and the baker. He interpreted their dreams only to be forgotten for 2 1/2 years.

When he was finally remembered and set free in the house of

Pharaoh, he had no grudges or unforgiveness. By now, a lot of people would be looking for Potiphar's wife to get even but not Joseph. Joseph is restored and promoted in the house of Pharaoh. Joseph gets married and named his first child, Manasseh, which literally means *"God made me forget all my toil in my father's house."*

Joseph had made a quality decision to close the gate on the injustice dealt toward him from his brothers. Then he was given a second child and he named him, Ephraim, which literally means, *"God made me fruitful."* Before Joseph was fruitful, he had to get past the hurt and the offenses. He had to close the gate. Joseph was not only set free from a literal prison he was also set free from the bruise. The life of Joseph is a great lesson and an example for all of us to follow.

We must not only close the gate on all the injustice done to us by others, but we must close the gate on the past mistakes and failures of our own doing. God wants to do a new thing in our lives. In order for God to do the new thing, we must turn loose of our old thing. It is exciting to know that my latter years will be greater than my former years. I have learned to wake up every day of my life with great expectation because in order to maintain my liberty, I have chosen to close the gate on the past.

5) Allow God to Touch Your Heart.

We hear a lot about touching the heart of God. We hear about being touched by an angel. We talk about when our hearts are touched by God. I'm not talking about becoming a Christian. I'm talking about a soft heart and a heart that is pure and compassionate. **A hardened heart is a deceptive heart**. A hardened heart keeps us from seeing and hearing things clearly. It also hinders us from speaking and acting in a compassionate manner. **One whose heart has been touched by God will be prompted to speak and act in a soft and compassionate way.**

We must allow our hearts to be touched by the need of those less fortunate. If you see someone in need such as a widow lady or a single mom who is going through a struggle you might be able to lighten their load in some manner. All around you are people that are hurting – people that need your love and encouragement. Maybe it's your husband or your wife or your child or your grandchild. **Don't miss the miracle of the moment.** Jesus said, *"When you do it to the least of these you do it unto me."* The Bible says in Proverbs, *"When you give to those in need you are lending unto God."* When God touches your heart, maybe you can find a young person who has no role model in their life and you can befriend them or perhaps mentor someone and show them additional meanings of life. Or how about just doing random acts of kindness and service without expecting a return? Someone once said, ***"People don't care what you know, until they know that you care."***

I have discovered two blessings of the Kingdom when I have allowed God to touch my own heart.

First of all, I have found the more I engage myself in other people's needs whether they are family, friends or sometimes strangers, I experience more joy. I realize that when I become discouraged or get my feelings hurt, most of the time it is because I have focused on my own expectations, my own self and what I need. This will get a person down every time. When I am able to get the focus off my own life and focus on helping others with their lives, this brings me a greater measure of contentment and victory in my own life.

When God touches your heart:

- Be a blessing
- Fill a need
- Heal a hurt

I like what John Bunyan, the author of The Pilgrim's Progress said: *"You have not lived today until you have done something for someone who cannot pay you back."* Expect nothing from others and allow the Lord to be your rewarder.

The second blessing you will experience when you allow God to touch your heart is the grace to fight a good fight, finish your course and endure to the end. This is best explained when you look at the life of David Livingstone.

David Livingstone was born in Scotland on March 19, 1813. He was a uniquely well equipped missionary and explorer. It was his religious faith that drew him to a career as a missionary. As it turned out, his achievements and exploration would surpass his missionary successes. Livingstone trained at the London Missionary Society and specialized in medicine. He was moved by a mentor and friend, Robert Moffett, who told him, "I have sometimes seen the morning sun and stood on a hill and saw the smoke of 1,000 villages where no missionary has ever been." His first trip to South Africa began in December 1840.

In 1843, Livingstone shot a lion. Before it died, however, the lion attacked Livingstone costing him the use of his left arm. Yet, his vision was not dimmed. He spent 33 years in Africa traveling over 40,000 miles attempting to reach the tribes who had not heard the name of Jesus.

While he was away in darkest Africa, back home in London,

Livingstone was considered lost and possibly dead. Henry Morton Stanley, a staff reporter for the New York Herald, was sent to look for the explorer and missionary. It took Stanley just over a year to find Livingstone. His comically understated words upon meeting the explorer, "Dr. Livingstone, I presume?" are now familiar to everyone.

Prior to his death in May 1873, Livingstone had been in poor health for several months. His crew had gone away to get supplies, and came back to find him in a kneeling position. His crew, as well as the tribesmen, had been very careful to never disturb him while he was, "praying to his God." Finally, after a few hours they decided to address him and found him still on his knees. However, he was dead. He had died on his knees praying to his God.

England wanted Livingstone to be shipped back to London for a memorial and proper burial. An argument pursued for eight months between England and the tribesmen of Africa concerning the remains of Livingstone. Finally, the tribesmen of Africa relented and gave up Livingstone's body. Before they shipped the body off to London, they cut out the heart of David Livingstone. They attached a note to his body which read, "You can have his body but his heart belongs to Africa." Even today, if you visit the city of Zambia, you can see the memorial to David Livingstone where his heart was buried beneath a tree. Attached to the tree is a sign that reads, "Here lies the heart of a man touched by God."[3]

The point is, when we allow our heart to be touched by God, we are more dedicated, faithful and determined to fulfill our vision, our destiny and God's call upon our lives.

The Bible tells us in Proverbs 4:23 – *"Keep your heart with all diligence for out of it flows the issues of life."* In Proverbs 17:22

it reads that, *"A merry heart does good like a medicine."* When we put it all together, we can say that when we keep our heart and allow God to touch it, our heart remains merry and is good like a medicine to us emotionally, physically and spiritually. This is a key that helps me maintain my liberty from the bruise.

Chapter 20 – Family and Siblings-Later Years

When I was 15 years old, I had the opportunity to see my biological mother but I refused. In later years, I certainly regretted my decision because I never had the opportunity again. I have reason to believe she moved to the Bay Area in California. There is a record of an individual with her name, born in the same month, who passed away in Santa Clara, California. To my knowledge, none of my brothers and sisters saw her once she moved from the Visalia area.

Mauren continued drinking until he passed away in 1976 in Porterville, California. During his last days he lived in a nursing home where we had the opportunity to visit and introduce Christa and Angela to him – Christa was age 6 and Angela was age 5.

Uncle Ralph passed away in December of 1976 – a few months after Mauren. To our knowledge he wasn't sick – he simply went to sleep and didn't wake up. He was a wonderful man and the only real father I ever had.

Aunt Ruth lived alone in her home in Cameron Creek for several years after Uncle Ralph passed away. Although I drove down on a monthly basis to visit her, after a few years it became apparent she needed to live with family.

When she was diagnosed with Alzheimer's, Judy and I insisted that she come to Roseville and live with us. This was a very difficult decision for her – she loved her home, her garden and her independence. One day when I was visiting her, I said, "When I was unable to take care of myself, you took care of me. Now it's my turn to take care of you."

After a period of time in our home, she settled down and came to believe she was back in her own home. She enjoyed attending church with us and was always treated with love and respect by our church family. On December 19, 1996, she passed away. Her funeral service was held in Cameron Creek Church where she had attended for 50 years. She was laid to rest alongside Uncle Ralph in Exeter, California. Aunt Ruth was my rescuer and my heroine. Without her intervention, I don't know where I would be today.

From the time I was five years old until I was nine, I knew about my sister Darlene but didn't actually have a relationship with her. This was due to my young age and the fact that she left home to go live with our maternal grandparents when she was a teenager.

I recall seeing pictures of her and thought she was the most beautiful girl I had ever seen. I remember seeing a picture of her in a roller skating outfit – in my mind she was like a movie star. In later years, Gwen and I saw Darlene and her family on a regular basis. By then she was married to Joe Danisi, a real gentleman that I came to admire. They were blessed with two lovely daughters, Rosalie and Juli.

I was quite young when Dale left home to join the Navy. Because of this, I have few memories of the years when he was at home.. Although we haven't seen one another very often in our adult years, I miss him and love him very much. He has a fine family and resides in Northern California with his wife, Tommie.

I have very few memories of Charles. I know that he spent a

lot of time with our biological father and some have speculated that Charles learned to drink at a very young age. In his later years he became an alcoholic and died of cancer at the age of 62.

Gwen and I were blessed to be able to be in the same home and have a normal brother-sister bond. She graduated from high school, worked for a few years and then married a wonderful man, Ford Tucker. I couldn't have asked for a better husband for Gwen – all who knew Ford loved him. He passed away in 2012. Ford and Gwen had one son – Chad. Gwen and I remain close and keep in regular contact with one another.

Laura was two years older than me. It seemed as though I barely had time to become acquainted with her before the family began to disintegrate. As a teenager, the children's protective agency became responsible for her and she was placed in foster care.

During my years in college, Laura and I renewed our relationship. By that time, she had a live-in boyfriend and they resided in the same city where I was going to college. Two or three times each week I would drop by her house and we would have a sandwich together while we watched a TV program.

Laura and her boyfriend were together for a few years and eventually they had two sons. When they separated, Laura kept the two little boys with her. Not long after that period, I lost regular contact with her. I would see her from time to time but she had turned to alcohol and that lifestyle eventually contributed to her sons being placed in foster care.

Her sons came back to her after they became adults. She

passed away in 2011 with her sons and her grandchildren at her bedside. Judy and I were able to be with her during her final hours.

Louise was taken in by Aunt Ruth's sister, Naomi and her husband, Truman. When Louise grew up and got married, they gave her a lovely wedding. Her first marriage didn't work out, but she eventually found a wonderful Christian man named Leon Gardner. Leon had a son from a previous marriage and later Louise and Leon had a son together – Leland. Currently, they live in Anaheim, California. We don't visit one another as often as we would like but I will never forget the little playmate of my childhood. Louise and I were the youngest and nearest to death but God brought us through.

Epilogue

Judy and I now reside in Lincoln, California – 8 miles from Roseville. We are blessed with 7 grandchildren – Ashley, Danielle, Caelan, Sophia, Aidan, Victoria and Annalise. One of our greatest delights in life is helping attend to the needs of our family, especially the grandchildren.

Our son-in-law, Don Proctor and our daughter, Christa, continue to serve as lead pastors in the church that Judy and I previously pastored. It is now Impact Church. Our faithful friends, The Quezadas, The Cagles, The Taylors and The Shenefields still serve alongside Don and Christa along with many other dedicated families. Art Quezada Sr., Joe Glasgow, Don Hamlett and Lori Austin have gone on to their reward and are now part of the great cloud of witnesses. We look forward to that day when we shall see them once again.

Our daughter, Angela, currently works as a State Park Ranger at Folsom Lake and our son-in-law, Marc, works for the Sacramento City Police Department.

On any given Sunday, when I am not speaking at other churches or traveling out of the country on behalf of Four Corners Ministries, you will find me in faithful attendance at Impact Church where Judy and I continue to serve as part of the pastoral team. I am often asked to fill the pulpit at Impact Church. I do love to minister so I always say "Yes" when asked. We greatly enjoy supporting this next generation as they step up to fulfill their God-given destiny.

Since my birth on September 18, 1945 I have learned this one thing: It is only in Jesus and His grace that I live and move and have my being. Through any failures, faults, and mistakes, we can always make a comeback because Jesus will never leave us or forsake us. I agree with the words of the Apostle Paul who wrote, *"I have not yet apprehended but this one thing I do, I forget those things which are behind and I press towards the mark of the high calling of God in Christ Jesus."*

Source Notes

1. Hamblen, Stuart. *How Big is God*

2. Tenney, Tommy. *The God Chasers.* Destiny Image Publishers, 1998

3. Various Publications including Wikipedia.org

Photo Gallery

My biological mother, Doris
at Age 18

Aunt Ruth Approximate Age 40

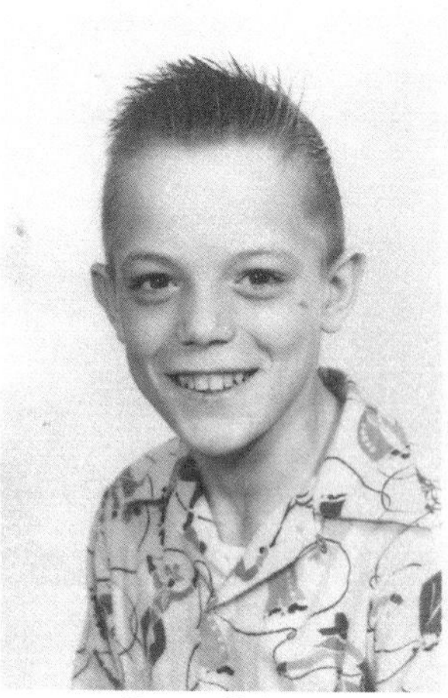

Russell Age 10

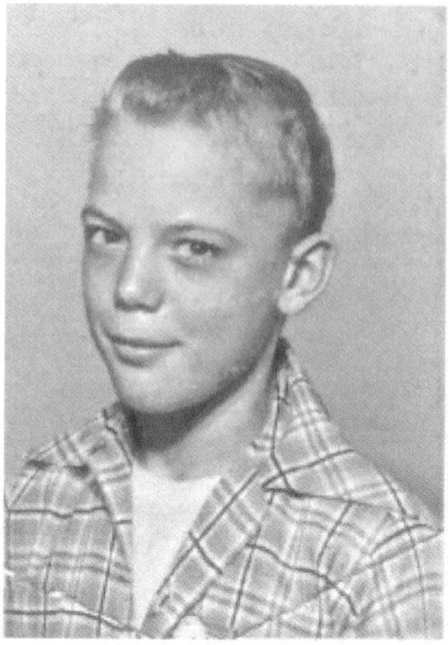

Russell Age 13

Russell Age 15

Dale Age 2 – Darlene Age 4

Charles Age 15

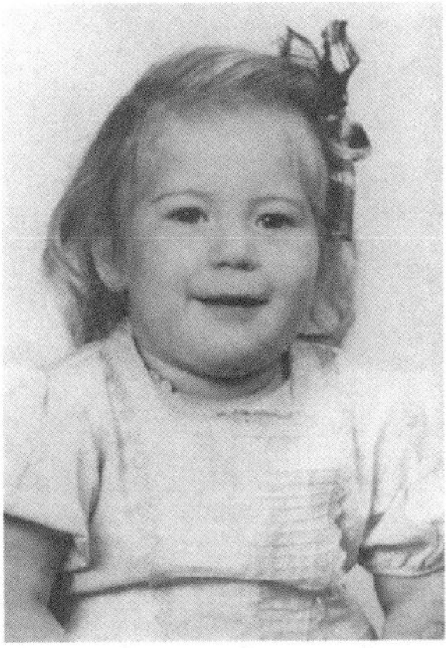
Gwen Approximate Age 3

Laura Approximate Age 14

Louise Approximate Age 7

Russell and Gwen - 1963

Ralph and Ruth McCollough Family – 1965

Russell at the Finish Line
1965

Russell and Judy
December 23, 1967

Russell – 1968

Roseville Gospel Tabernacle
100 Lincoln Street, Roseville, CA

Roseville Gospel Tabernacle Choir – December 1969
Russell – back row, left
Judy – front row, third from left
Dwight, Choir Director – front row, left

Russell and Judy - 1979

Christa Age 8 – Angela Age 7

New Church Building – 8330 Brady Lane, Roseville, CA

First service in new church – Russell takes a backward flip off the platform as promised

Russell and Judy – Dedication Service – November 1992

Current Family Photos

Russell and Judy McCollough

Don and Christa Proctor
Danielle, Sophia, Victoria, Annalise

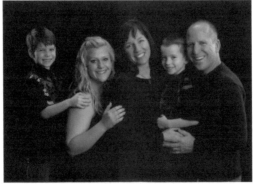

Marc and Angela Milligan
Ashley, Caelan and Aidan

Deception of Disease Ad

If you enjoyed this book, we recommend:

You have

nothing

to lose

by believing.

Every life demands courage and faith.
What's YOUR mountain? You can *take* it!

Available at

Deception of
DISEASE
.com

Also available for Kindle & Nook

Come Back Stories Ad

We also recommend:

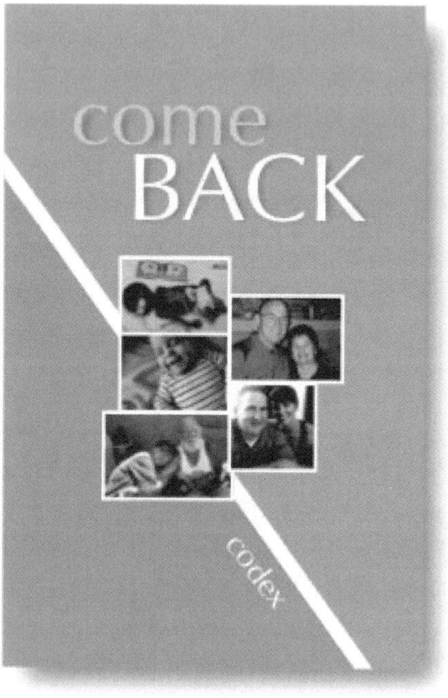

Extraordinary stories from ordinary people
who want to share HOPE with you.

Available FREE at
ImpactChurch.info (just cover S&H)
Also available FREE for Kindle & Nook

impact
CHURCH

Impact Church Media
www.impactchurch.info